JAZZ Life & Times

This is a series of books about jazz artists, all of whom have made either a significant contribution or have had an impact on the jazz scene. Unlike some jazz books that concentrate upon the detail of the performers' lives or music, this series is concerned with much more. Here can be seen the social background into which the subject was born and raised and the environment in which his or her music was formed. The social, domestic, racial and commercial pressures that shaped the person are examined alongside an assessment of other musicians who may have influenced the artist or been influenced by them. Of course, the music is not overlooked and each book carries a discographical essay in which the artist's recorded output is summarized and analyzed. Well-illustrated, the Life & Times series of books is an important and long overdue addition to jazz literature.

Bunk Johnson

HIS
LIFE & TIMES

CHRISTOPHER HILLMAN

UNIVERSE BOOKS
New York

FOR BILL RUSSELL AND KARL GERT ZUR HEIDE

In the same illustrated series:
Louis Armstrong by Mike Pinfold
Dizzy Gillespie by Barry McRae
Billie Holiday by John White
B B King by Howard Elson
Gene Krupa by Bruce Crowther
Bud Powell by Alan Groves
Fats Waller by Alyn Shipton

First published in Britain in 1988 by
SPELLMOUNT LTD.
Tunbridge Wells, Kent, England

Published in the United States of
America in 1988 by
UNIVERSE BOOKS
381 Park Avenue South,
New York, N.Y. 10016.

© Christopher Hillman 1988

**Library of Congress Cataloging in
Publication Data**
Hillman, Christopher
  Bunk Johnson, his life and times.
  (Jazz life and times)
  Bibliography: p. 144
  Includes index.
  1. Johnson, Bunk, 1879-1949. 2.
Jazz musicians — United States —
Biography. I. Title. II. Series.
ML419.J6H5 1988   788′.1′0924 [B]
87-35765
ISBN 0-87663-685-7
ISBN 0-87663-745-4 (pbk.)

Designed by: Words & Images,
Speldhurst, Tunbridge Wells, Kent
Typeset by: Vitaset,
Paddock Wood, Kent
Printed & bound in Great Britain by
Anchor Brendon Ltd., Tiptree, Essex

CONTENTS

ACKNOWLEDGEMENTS

The pictures in this book come from the Max Jones Collection, Jazz Music Books, the *Melody Maker*, William Russell, Terry Dash, *Footnote* magazine, Mike Casimir, *Paragon Limited Edition Records*, and Festa New Orleans Music Productions, Ascona. The illustrations are reproduced by permission. Every effort has been made by the publishers to trace copyright holders, and they apologise to anyone whose name may inadvertently have been omitted from this list.

PREFACE

This is not intended to be an exhaustive biography of Bunk Johnson. Such a work would require a great deal of original research, both in the field and among book-lined shelves, and, starting from scratch, would very likely be impossible at this late date. It would also have to be a very focussed work, severely eschewing self-indulgent analysis of musical trends and the less directly relevant aspects of the story of jazz and of the New Orleans background. I have done no original research, relying for all my information on what has already been published in one form or another. Some of the documentation is readily accessible and already well known to jazz enthusiasts. Some is less easily found, in obscure and long-discontinued publications; but it is all there for one who knows, or is well advised, where to look. Much is at least second-hand, and is the work of committed, and generally thorough and well-informed, enthusiasts to rationalise existing information in order to present the stories of the musicians from the collective memories of their contemporaries. For the source material of many of these, we are in the debt of the William Ransom Hogan Jazz Archive at Tulane University and its dedicated archivist, Richard B. Allen.

I have tried to correlate all the information about Bunk Johnson, and other musicians who throw light on him, that I could find in print. A certain amount of selection has occurred, and some events and anecdotes which seemed spurious or had an aura of the apocryphal about them have not been included. A good deal of the information about Bunk is open to question, or at least interpretation, and I have tried to show, unambiguously, where this is the case. There are many loose ends, as well as trails which it could well be rewarding to follow to their destination, but time and space forbid me to indulge in that pleasure here. I have included some, possible fanciful, analysis of Bunk's convoluted character and have tried, in an inevitably ineffectual way, to see the events of his life through his own eyes as well as from the point of view of a detached enthusiast.

In the life of Bunk Johnson, major events such as the two world wars and the Depression take on a very limited importance. He was, perhaps more than any other, a musician living in the half-world of his own choosing, relating only to others of his own kind and the fellow travellers who attach themselves to his profession. In his self-absorption, he was not even much interested in the wider aspects of his own calling. It is necessary, however, to place him in the context of jazz as a whole, both as a style of music and a way of life, and that has been my main endeavour.

It has also been necessary to evaluate the effect on the development of jazz, particularly New Orleans jazz, and the well-being of its practitioners, of the Enthusiast, that strange embodiment of good-will, scholarship, determination and wishful-thinking, among the ranks of whom I must, gladly but humbly, count myself. It was an enthusiast, Tom Bethell, who, with much original research, compiled the book about George Lewis upon which I have relied heavily for much of my factual matter; another, Donald M. Marquis, provided in his book about Buddy Bolden a resolution of the inconsistencies in Bunk's own account of his early life. Enthusiasts have generated virtually all the writings, not all directly relevant but invariably fascinating and enlightening, that I have scanned during my study, as well as most of the recordings of the music.

In my searches and wonderings I have been most generously helped by my friends, enthusiastic and expert, Charlie Crump, Roy Middleton, Mike Tovey and Alan Ward. Most of all, of course, anyone with any interest in Bunk Johnson must acknowledge a debt to William Russell, Eugene Williams and their collaborators. Gene is, sadly, no longer with us but Bill lives on in New Orleans, surrounded by paper, records and memories. If anyone is to write a proper biography of Bunk, Bill Russell is uniquely equipped through his personal knowledge of the man and his involvement in his career; so in a different way, is Paul A. Larsen, who has made the trumpeter his lifetime's study. If those two were to get together, what a book we would have. In the meantime . . .

INTRODUCTION

The story of Bunk Johnson is one of the most extraordinary in the history of jazz. He was born early enough to have played with some of the men considered responsible for the rise of the music, and, having gained a considerable reputation in and around his headquarters of New Orleans in his prime, he fell into obscurity. He was subsequently rediscovered, and his second career brought him considerable acclaim in New York. It is a tale to which an element of romance must inevitably attach itself, and one in which by no means all is what it seems. It has its disagreeable aspects as well as its glorious ones, and it needs a good deal of disentangling; but it is an important story and has to be placed in its proper context, which is that of jazz as a whole. It must also be seen against the background of the Negro's place in American society and culture and his part in the initiation and development of jazz, the most significant and original flowering of artistic expression in the history of America.

Of all the notable figures in the story of jazz, Willie 'Bunk' Johnson is perhaps the most misunderstood, and he himself, through his exasperating nature, was partly to blame. So were those who most wished him well, the amateur musicologists who turned him into a symbol of something that existed only in their own imaginations. Most of all, however, Bunk was the victim, as well as the beneficiary, of history – of the extraordinarily compressed evolution of jazz over a few decades and the commercial pressures resulting from its widespread popularity.

By the time Bunk Johnson embarked on his second career, New Orleans had ceased to be the centre of jazz. It had reached a wider public in Chicago and New York through the efforts of some distinguished musicians and notorious entrepreneurs, many of them from the Crescent City. From being an urban folk music it had, in the 1930s, in the form of swing, become the prime style of popular music in the western world. It had also, of course, become big business.

Until the late 1930s jazz, at least in the North, had always been commercial music. The euphoria following World War I had given James Reese Europe, former leader of the Hellfighters military band, the opportunity to found the Clef Club, a centre for negro musicians, in New York. From this, and from the existing popularity of vaudeville and minstrel performers, came the impact of blues singers on the New York recording scene, promoted by such figures as the singer and bandleader Perry Bradford and the self-styled 'Father of the Blues', W. C. Handy. While their records were, originally, aimed at the growing negro market in the North, they also appealed to the white audience, which craved something a little less 'polite' than what had hitherto been available. Records were produced solely to make money, although most of those responsible for the product, being musicians, did ensure that a reasonable standard of expertise and artistry prevailed.

Cut-throat competition was the order of the day, and record companies made 'cover' versions of their rivals' successes, a state of affairs that continued until the height of the swing era. The Depression resulted in a thinning of their ranks, but the companies, and also the bandleaders that survived did so very successfully indeed, supplying a young audience which had grown immense by the development of radio. Meanwhile, the impoverished Negroes were catered for by their own 'race' records, mainly an updated, urban form of blues reverting to the folk music of earlier times. It was the ubiquity, in the popular media of the 1930s, of the large swing bands that made some of the more analytical buyers of records (items which were then becoming collectable on a less ephemeral basis) start to take an interest in the music of the earlier decade, and also in its practitioners. Some of the latter had been swallowed up by the big bands, others were scuffling for an existence in the hinterland and some had disappeared altogether.

Part of the impetus for the enthusiasts' movement came from Europe, where visiting American musicians – notably Negroes who found the social climate rewarding – had inspired and intrigued the local intellectuals. One of these, the Frenchman Hugues Panassié, paved the way by producing records in America. He looked back to the music of King Oliver and assembled a band he thought capable of reproducing this sound; eclectically, the results were not a success, but the music which came out of his sessions was very worthwhile. Shortly afterwards, attention was directed to New Orleans itself. In 1940 the journalist Heywood Hale Broun recorded a band featuring the almost mythical trumpet player Kid Rena. The results were crude, both technically and musically, but there was a warm, earthy ambience that contrasted affectively with the brash, mechanical sounds of swing. The early Blue Note recordings featuring such performers as Sidney Bechet in an informal small-group setting were ample proof of the lack of spontaneity, soul and 'purity' of much big-band music, where arrangers removed all the freedom of expression upon which the best sort of jazz had thrived.

This was a very over-simplified point of view, considered in the light of what Duke Ellington, Count Basie and even the 'King of Swing', Benny Goodman, were achieving. The 'noble savage', however, is an attractive concept to the intelligentsia, and the idea of New Orleanians as a breed of men who played as they felt, were free of undue commercial pressures, and were able to conjure up startlingly momentous emotional expressiveness without ever indulging in anything so vulgar as technical display, became the antidote to the imagined decline of jazz into a mass-produced, sterile product. The truth, as far as we shall ever be able to define it, was much less extreme.

The movement to promote pure New Orleans music needed a hero. In the recollections of Louis Armstrong, himself enmeshed in big-band showmanship at that time, and others who were canvassed, the name of Bunk Johnson kept cropping up as somebody special. He was run to earth in New Iberia, Louisiana, where he had been vegetating for some years, given a new set of teeth and a trumpet, and recorded with a band of New Orleans musicians. The recordings stimulated either a very positive emotional response or baffled superiority, but they generated enough interest to get Bunk and his band to New York, and received considerable acclaim from a wider array of enthusiasts.

Ironically, about the same time as Bunk made his impact on New York, some other musicians were reacting against swing in their own way. This had nothing to do with any 'golden age' or with the promptings of opinionated enthusiasts. Dizzie Gillespie and Charlie Parker provided an alternative sort of spontaneity, but a very complex and musicianly sort. Once the audiences got over their surprise at these independent displays, they divided into camps and started throwing stones at each other. The traditionalists and the modernists could never agree, but neither could they agree to differ. To the former, bebop was not jazz at all, or even anything worth listening to; to the latter, Bunk's music was a manifestation of things long superseded, played by worn-out men who had never been much good anyway. Those who were not inclined to these extremes could not avoid over-reacting to the fervour of both points of view, hearing Bunk's music as an archaic noise and bebop as an anarchic noise.

It was Bunk Johnson's tragedy that not only was he the hero of the traditionalists, to them he *was* New Orleans music. While there were plenty of musicians left in the city and others from the heyday of the 1920s still playing true to their tradition in the North, he, along with his band, was the only one achieving much prominence at that time. He became the figure-head of a movement towards a sort of mythical simplicity with which his own strong and articulate views on music-making were not, in fact, in accord. The enthusiasts tended to turn a deaf ear to his musical ambitions when such ambitions did not concur with their own views; in historical matters, however, they treated him as a sage, a role he was far too self-centred to fulfil.

Bunk Johnson has suffered from the view of many influential jazz commentators – that New Orleans had become a backwater containing only those musicians who had not had the talent to make their way in the North during the 1920s. There were, however, many reasons why some chose to remain at home, or to make a living in unceremonious circumstances away from the big time. Bunk, like many others, was not an organisation man, and he was an extreme individualist. Many are the names of legendary musicians who never recorded, but who are remembered with admiration or even awe by their fellows. The styles of some we can reconstruct from the common elements in the playing of men who claim to have been influenced by them, while those of others remain a mystery only capable of evaluation from their subjective and possibly romantic reputations. These musicians provide a tantalising spice to jazz history, and a salutary reminder that our retrospective judgement can be only partial at best.

In Bunk Johnson we are fortunate to have two musicians in one. Firstly there is the legendary associate of the founding fathers of jazz and the seminal influence on later luminaries, who was left behind in the tidal movement of the music towards the North; and secondly there is the grand old man, fortuitously and lovingly brought out of obscurity to remind the world of how he used to play. It is possible to insult him by asserting that he would have fared better in the annals of jazz had he never reappeared, and that his sad, senile stumblings do no justice to the musician he professed, and others claimed him, to be. It is also possible to find in his playing a remarkable vitality and warmth which go a long way to compensate for a naive musicality and a waning technique. Both these points of view result from a far too superficial assessment of his actual performance on recordings. There is, indeed, along with some of the limitations of technique to be expected, a force remarkable in an elderly man; but there is a vindication of his claim to have affected the course of jazz through his influence on later men, and some evidence that, by being one of the first artistically and socially sophisticated jazz musicians, he directed the course of the music during its most formative years. If this assessment is correct, and if there is any sort of linear development in jazz from its beginnings to what it is now and what it is to become, then, for the light that he throws on the music as a whole, a musician in such a seminal or pivotal position must be of interest far beyond his own immediate story.

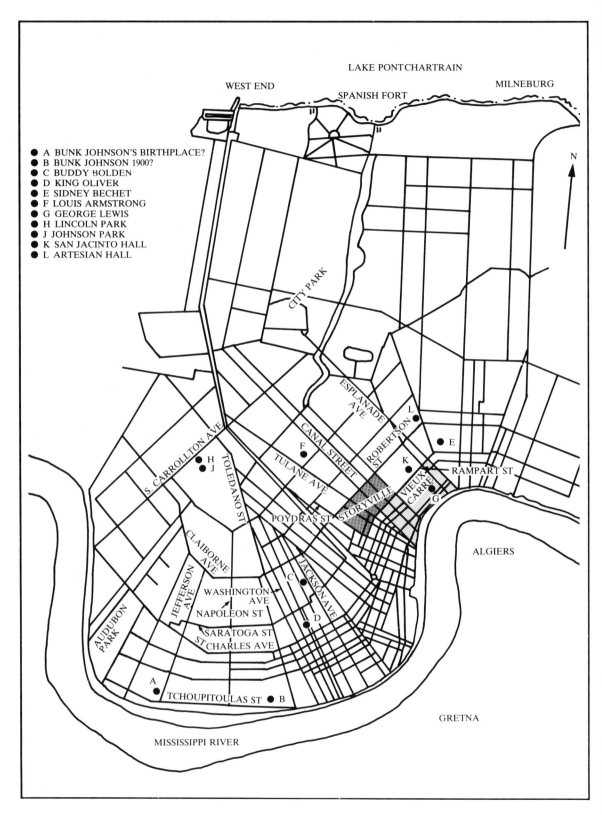

- A BUNK JOHNSON'S BIRTHPLACE?
- B BUNK JOHNSON 1900?
- C BUDDY BOLDEN
- D KING OLIVER
- E SIDNEY BECHET
- F LOUIS ARMSTRONG
- G GEORGE LEWIS
- H LINCOLN PARK
- J JOHNSON PARK
- K SAN JACINTO HALL
- L ARTESIAN HALL

LAKE PONTCHARTRAIN

WEST END   SPANISH FORT   MILNEBURG

N

CITY PARK

ESPLANADE AVE

ROBERTSON ST

S. CARROLLTON AVE

TOLEDANO ST

CANAL STREET

TULANE AVE

RAMPART ST

POYDRAS ST   STORYVILLE   VIEUX CARRE

ALGIERS

CLAIBORNE AVE

JEFFERSON AVE

JACKSON AVE

WASHINGTON AVE

NAPOLEON ST

SARATOGA ST

ST CHARLES AVE

AUDUBON PARK

TCHOUPITOULAS ST   B

GRETNA

MISSISSIPPI RIVER

CHAPTER 1

HISTORY IS BUNK

In evaluating Bunk Johnson's historical claims, we must take account of the circumstances under which they were made. Prior to his rediscovery in 1938, the pioneer enthusiasts had visited New Orleans and spoken to several experienced musicians. The enthusiasts' initial interest in Bunk was from an archival point of view, since they had little faith in his ability to play the trumpet in public. In him, since he was a much less reticent talker than the average musician, they felt that they had the ideal means to fill the gaps in their knowledge. Bunk, who said he had been born in 1879, must, as they thought, have been in at the very beginnings of jazz, and the facts as he told them were treated as gospel truth. They marvelled at his memory and credited him with an articulate understanding of what they wanted as well as an objective, almost academic, outlook to match their own. His appearance, worthy of an *eminence grise*, and his ability to charm only added to his credibility.

In fact, Bunk had a considerable axe to grind. He was determined to forge a new career and to present his principles of music-making to the world. While there may have been some altruism in his mission, it was mainly self-centred, designed to capitalise on the reputation that his name had created. It is difficult to see him as mercenary, for he spent money as soon as he received it, largely on drink. He was, however, ruthlessly opportunistic by nature and heedless of the feelings of others or the professional obligations of his calling. He had, despite a lifetime of loose living and a good deal of hard manual labour, a splendid constitution, and, for all that he tended to live in a world of his own, he still had all his wits about him. The provenance of his nickname is not clear. Some claimed that it related to what came out of his mouth, particularly when he was drunk; but Louis Armstrong said that it was a pleasure just to listen to him talk.

Map of New Orleans

Apart from Bunk himself, the principal musician in the minds of those who sought his version of jazz history was Buddy Bolden, remembered as a colossus by most of the men they had consulted in New Orleans. Bunk could gain an advantage in their estimation, both as an interesting musician and a credible historian, by establishing an association with the legendary cornettist who, whether or not he was the first to invest the negro music of New Orleans with a 'hot' characteristic, made an unforgettable impression on a great many people by the power of his playing.

Charles 'Buddy' Bolden, born in 1877, was the most popular musician in the city during the period between 1900 and 1906, and the prime exponent of an exciting new style. Bolden's band evolved during the second half of the 1890s and by the turn of the century its style and personnel were settled: on trombone was Willie Cornish, still using the valved instrument, but able to match his leader in strength; Frank Lewis and Willie Warner were on clarinets, Jefferson 'Brock' Mumford played guitar, Jimmy Johnson, bass, and either Henry Zeno or Cornelius Tillman, drums. The band's approach was in direct contrast to that of the educated Creole musicians, such as John Robichaux and Manuel Perez, who had previously dominated the musical life of New Orleans. It was therefore extremely popular with the rank-and-file black population, which up to that time had had little formal outlet for its musical aspirations beyond the crude neighbourhood string bands and the singing in the churches.

Buddy Bolden was a man of great appetites, particularly for drink and for women, who idolised him. At the height of his popularity, in 1906, his actions and moods became unpredictable and often violent, and he had difficulty holding his band together. He fired the faithful Cornish, Mumford and Johnson, taking on in their places Frankie Dusen, Lorenzo Staultz and Bob Lyons. At times he used a lot of different musicians, accounting for at least some of the legion who claimed to have played with him, several of whom remembered him as difficult, or at least eccentric. Eventually the running of the band fell to Dusen; often Bolden did not turn up, and his place was taken by, among others, Edward Clem. On one occasion when (as was often the case) he did not hand over the band's pay, Dusen told him, 'We don't need you any more.' By the end of 1906 Bolden had ceased playing altogether and, after further deterioration, he was committed to the Louisiana State Insane Asylum, where he remained until his death in 1931.

Bunk said that he was asked by Bolden to join his band in 1895, and that the other musicians were Willie Cornish, Willie Warner, Brock Mumford, Jimmy Johnson and Cornelius Tillman. A photograph of the Bolden band, still the only one known, was then produced by Cornish, and Bunk, when shown it, identified these same musicians (except for Tillman, who was not in the picture) and said that it was taken just before he joined. Other evidence, which confirms Bunk's identification (the photograph also includes Frank Lewis on clarinet) indicates that it was taken during the band's heyday, between 1903 and 1905. Jimmy Johnson is certainly not the eleven-year-old lad that his birth certificate, which has since been found, shows him to have been in 1895; and other facts brought forth by Bunk concerning Bolden and his children prove that he was acquainted with him during the later period.

Several musicians of the time have said that Bunk did not play with Bolden, who, according to all other recollections, never used a second cornet in his dance band and would have been wary of showing his tricks to a younger man. It is possible that Bunk played alongside Bolden on parades, and he may have substituted for him during the leader's final, erratic period. Bunk also played later with the Eagle Band, which Frankie Dusen formed around the remnants of Bolden's group.

It is interesting to note that some commentators, notably the Belgian writer Robert Goffin, were becoming sceptical about Bunk's stories even during his lifetime. New Orleans musicians related tales of Bunk coming and asking them about Bolden, and the clarinettist 'Big Eye' Louis Nelson Delisle for one, sent him off with a flea in his ear. Towards the end of his life Bunk became very reticent, declining to elaborate on his established spiel already published in Ramsey and Smith's book *Jazzmen*. His recollections, either heard on recordings or transcribed, have a bombastic poetry typical of the old-timer seeking to set himself in the centre of the story; they are best treated as romantic folk tales, artistic expressions complementary to his music. While they perfectly set the atmosphere of old New Orleans, to glean solid facts from them one must sift with care and offer them up against other, harder evidence.

Bunk's garbled and self-centred version of history provided the spur to a later generation of enthusiastic researchers, who, with much diligence and discipline, sought to set matters straight. One of these is Donald M. Marquis, whose exemplary study of Buddy Bolden's life analyses the inconsistencies in Bunk's story and comes to the conclusion that he added to his age about ten years.

William (or Willie, as he preferred it) Geary Johnson stated that he was born on 27th December 1879 on Laurel Street, between Peters Avenue and Octavia Street, in the uptown section of New Orleans. He said that he was one of 14 children, that his father was called William and his mother Theresa, and that they were ex-slaves. He was raised by his mother, a cook, near the intersection of Amelia Street with Tchoupitoulas Street, the long thoroughfare that runs along behind the docks and warehouses lining the Mississippi. Recent painstaking research by Lawrence Gushee has unearthed, in the Census of 1900, an entry for 3523 Tchoupitoulas Street, near the crossing in question: the head of the household is given as Theresa Johnson, aged 44 and other members as her daughter Roselia, aged 11, and a ten-year-old son whose name, in the thick, florid writing, could be either Geary or Gerry. Neither of these names was shown by Gushee's searches to be common in New Orleans at that time, and either could have been intended by the writer, since the information would have been obtained orally. The son's month of birth is given as December 1889, so, if this is our man, Marquis's ten-year estimate is spot on. Being a nice round number, it is also a believable fabrication.

The name of the one other person shown to be living in the household, which occupied half of the building, may be deciphered as Millie Young. The cornet player Charlie Love has stated that when he played in the Caddo Band in Shreveport in 1917 the trombonist, William Young, was Bunk's uncle. It is possible to construct various relationships linking this trombonist to the Johnsons. Millie might have been Theresa's elder sister, making William Young Bunk's cousin rather than his uncle; or, since there is no Mr Johnson mentioned, it is possible that Theresa had formed a new liaison with a somewhat younger man, and that Millie was her mother-in-law – either legally or common-law. The latter would make the claim of 'uncle' a believable prevarication. Alternatively, the Youngs may just have been friends close enough to justify the honorary title. None of this proves that the family in the Census is that of Bunk Johnson, but, taken along with other evidence and with the inconsistencies in Bunk's own story, it does seem very likely.

Bunk said that he was taught to play the cornet by Professor Wallace Cutchey, a native of Mexico City, at New Orleans University. He said, variously, that he learnt from Cutchey (probably a phonetic spelling of the name) at the age of seven or ten, that he left the university in 1894, and that he left school in 1894. Apparently the teacher was satisfied enough by his student's progress to persuade Theresa to buy him a cheap cornet, and evidently by the age of 14 Bunk considered himself ready to become a regular musician. His first notable job, which (with the ten-year adjustment) would have been in 1904 or 1905, was in the band of Adam Olivier, a second-rate cornettist and violinist who led a reading group – probably a lesser version of John Robichaux's band, until about 1910. Olivier, whose barber shop was close to Bunk's home, often played at Lincoln Park and is said to have lost his audiences to Bolden, who was able to summon them from the adjacent Johnson Park by playing louder. Olivier probably needed

18

little persuasion from Bunk that he should take on a hotter cornettist to strengthen the sound of his band. Bunk said that he joined Olivier as a step in the direction of playing with Bolden.

Whether or not Bunk knew it at the time, Adam Olivier's band was only a stepping-stone for him. Were it not for Bunk's recollections it would remain obscure indeed, just one among many neighbourhood bands playing for ordinary social occasions. It did have one other noteworthy member, however – the pianist Tony Jackson. Bunk alleged that he and Jackson were contemporaries and were raised in the same district, but in fact the pianist was 28 when he left New Orleans for the first time, in 1904. He joined the famous Whitman Sisters' touring show, but left them to make his way as a solo artist when they reached Louisville, Kentucky, and returned home the same autumn. He stayed until 1907, when he went to Chicago, and it is probably during that time that he and Bunk were together with Olivier. He was also in New Orleans between 1910 and 1912. Bunk recalled that Jackson worked in Lulu White's grand establishment, and claimed to have helped him to compose *Baby I'd love to steal you* in a back room at Johnny Lala's Big 25 Club; he reinforced this by whistling the piece (including the verse, which he said later musicians did not know) on a recording.

It is interesting to note, in his recollections, that Bunk often referred to musicians whose names, along with some details of their careers, were already known to the enthusiasts from other sources – in the case of Tony Jackson, who died in 1921, from the

Mahogany Hall, 1940s, once operated by Lulu White

reminiscences of Jelly Roll Morton. Whether Bunk knew that such names would make his tales more interesting, or whether his information was derived from the same sources, is an issue that should always be borne in mind when his testimony is unsupported. It is possible that he made much of a fleeting acquaintance with a musician from his own locality who had already become established as an interesting early figure. He may even have insinuated himself imaginatively into the Olivier band to pretend to a juxtaposition with such a man. Giving him the benefit of the doubt, he probably did work for Olivier's band (in itself no guarantee of historical distinction) and Jackson, who certainly played with the group occasionally, may well have coincided with Bunk for a while.

According to Bunk Johnson's own curriculum vitae, he played with Bolden from 1895 when he walked out on Olivier for more rewarding employment, until 1898, when he joined Bob Russell's band. He soon left the latter to return to Bolden because, he said, 'they could not play very much.' It is only through Bunk that Russell appears on the pages of jazz history, so his may have been an obscure amateur group with which Bunk played during his apprenticeship before working for Adam Olivier. When Bunk returned to Bolden, Frankie Dusen had replaced Willie Cornish on trombone. Bunk stayed for seven months and then set out on a series of wanderings which, while they cannot all be refuted, do not have the ring of truth about them. He claimed to have worked in an number of circuses, among them that of P. G. Loral, on liners travelling as far as Europe and Australia (on one occasion he said that he worked in England and played for Queen Victoria), and that he was back in New Orleans in 1900 playing in Tom Anderson's dance hall. He also said that he was in San Francisco in 1905. It seems most likely that such of these happenings as were based on fact occurred later, and that Bunk used tales supporting his absence from home to cover a period when, in actuality, he was too young to have appeared in other musicians' recollections.

Bunk said that he worked with Jelly Roll Morton in Hattie Rogers's sporting house in Storyville in 1903. He could not, as he claimed, have been in the Eagle Band at the time, since he only joined it after Morton left the New Orleans area in 1907; it is, in any case, unlikely that an immature black cornettist would have been allowed into a white bordello where Morton, an educated Creole and an elegant pianist, was welcome. Bunk also said that he played with Jelly in Gulfport, Mississippi, in 1903 or 1904, recalling jobs at the Great Southern Hotel and at Bumble Bee Park. Morton certainly spent some time in Gulfport, and adjacent Biloxi, before he ranged further afield. If these activities of Bunk's are based on fact, it seems he started his wanderings while still in his teens. He

The Superior Orchestra in 1910: (back row) Buddy Johnson, Bunk Johnson, 'Big Eye' Louis Nelson and Billy Marrero; (front row) Walter Brundy, Peter Bocage and Richard Payne

may well have encountered Jelly through their mutual friend Tony Jackson, but it must be borne in mind that Morton was a figure of considerable interest to the enthusiastic owing to the series of recordings for the Library of Congress which Alan Lomax had made of his playing and talking in 1938, and also that the pianist had died in 1941 and was thus unable to offer contradiction.

Bunk may have played with the Eagle Band on occasions as early as 1905 or 1906, probably when it was augmented for parade work, but he does not seem to have been a regular member at that time; his claim to have helped Joe Oliver with his playing when they were both with the group makes more sense in a brass-band context. It is not even clear when Bunk left Adam Olivier, but Peter Bocage remembered him in the Superior Orchestra in 1906 or 1907. The personnel, seen on a photo of the band taken in 1908 when Bocage was 21, shows Bunk, Big Eye Nelson (clarinet), Buddy Johnson (trombone), Richard Payne (guitar), Billy Marrero (double bass), Walter Brundy (drums) and Bocage (violin). Bunk's appearance is youthful, to say the least. Pops Foster first came across Bunk playing with the Superior at a picnic at the Fairgrounds in 1908, with the same personnel apart from René Baptiste on guitar. Foster was in Manuel Perez' band, John Robichaux occupied the Pavilion and the Superior was playing on

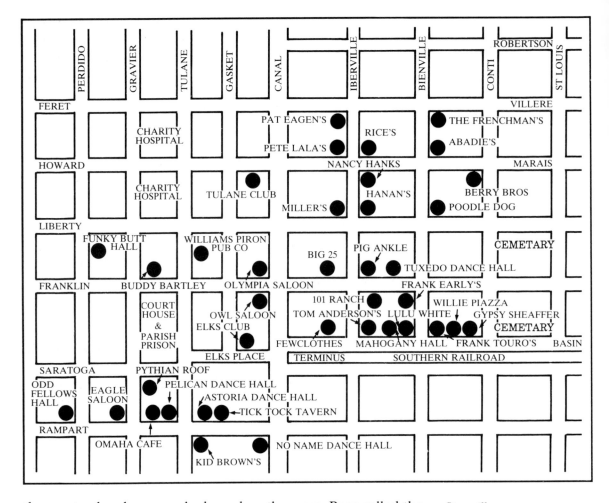

Storyville

the racetrack, where people danced on the grass. Pops called the Superior a ragtime band, and Bocage endorsed this, saying that they played from music and implying, elsewhere, that he helped Bunk with his reading. Both Bocage and Foster were full of praise for Bunk's playing, saying that he was 'a nice soft trumpet player, stylish, with a beautiful tone.'

Pops Foster remembered that Bunk started drinking heavily and was fired by the Superior Orchestra, so he joined the rough-and-ready Eagle in whose company such behaviour was the norm. The band's headquarters the Eagle Saloon, on Gravier Street in the black District, and Pops said that Bunk virtually lived there, sleeping on the pool table. In his time, the other musicians were Dusen, Mumford, Henry Zeno on drums, Dandy Lewis on bass, and a young clarinettist who was to become famous. Sidney Bechet taught himself to play clarinet after the example of Big Eye Nelson Alphonse Picou and George Baquet, who was impressed enough by his precocious talent to give him some lessons. Sidney started playing in his brother Leonard's band, the Silver Bells. Leonard was studying to be a dentist, so he was not entirely single-minded about music, and he started the band mainly to keep his younger brother out of trouble. Leonard played trombone, but he also dabbled with the clarinet until Sidney started playing it much better than he could.

Although, in keeping with his mother's wishes, Leonard kept trying to make Sidney stay with the Silver Bells, the adolescent prodigy seems to have been able to work occasionally, on account of Baquet's patronage, with the city's finest musicians from around 1907. He and the cornettist Buddy Petit, who was the same age, organised the Young Olympia band in 1908 or 1909, much to Leonard's dismay; he also seems to have played occasionally with John Robichaux and Freddie Keppard. Later, when he was back under his brother's wing, Bunk Johnson played a job with the Silver Bells, and, according to Leonard, enticed Sidney away. Bunk promised their mother that he would look after Sidney, and apparently he was as good as his word; Sidney recalled: 'Bunk was the quietest man, even with all his drinking. He's been around a long time, but nobody ever did know where he'd come from.' Bechet is said to have played with Joe Oliver and Jack Carey in 1913. From 1914 to 1917, when he left the area, he generally worked outside New Orleans, though he did perform with Oliver in 1916. It is not clear when he left the Eagle Band, or who replaced him.

Another famous musician who played with the Eagle Band during Bunk's stay was Warren 'Baby' Dodds. He learnt the drums from Dave Perkins, a great early expert, and played some parades with Bunk, possibly in the augmented Eagle Band. He then studied with Walter Brundy of the Superior Orchestra, who taught him many techncial aspects of drumming as well as to read music. When Henry Zeno died suddenly it was Dodds who was asked to replace him. According to Dodds, Frankie Dusen was part American Indian, with a reddish complexion, and he played the trombone rather like Kid Ory, but more smoothly. The younger musicians were beginning to favour the slide trombone, but Dusen seems to have preferred the valved instrument. Nevertheless, Dodds said that he played in the 'tailgate' style, so called on account of the positioning of the trombonist over the tailgate of a band wagon to make room for his instrument's slide; the term is descriptive of the long glissandos which became a feature of the classic New Orleans style. Later Dusen was called to Los Angeles by Jelly Roll Morton, but his valve trombone was considered so old-fashioned there that he soon went back home in disgust. Pops Foster said that the Eagle's leader was the only man of whom Bunk was frightened when he was drinking, because Dusen would beat him with a strap to keep him in order. Pops did say, though, that

Bunk was a very nice guy when he was not drinking.

It is not clear whether Bunk continued to play regularly with the Eagles up to the time he left New Orleans; Pops Foster implies that eventually even they ran out of patience with his drunkenness. He certainly did have other jobs; he recalled playing in the 'tonks' of Dago Tony and Pete Lala when the Eagles did not have a gig (the former, under its previous proprietor, 'Mustache', had been a haunt of Bolden's). The Eagles' big night was Saturday, when they played at Masonic Hall, but they were also in demand for many other functions – for dances and, in their larger form, for parades and funerals. Lee Collins, born in 1901, considered Bunk the best jazz musician in the city and took him as his model. When the Eagles played at Funkey Butt Hall, close to his home, he would sit on the bandstand beside his idol. He learnt quickly, and was asked to substitute for Bunk when he was 'off on another of his famous drunks.' Lee knew the band's repertoire and was delighted to be told that he had captured Bunk's tone and feeling. Collins bought his first cornet from a pawn shop at the age of 13, so it seems that Bunk was associated with the Eagles, at least intermittently, as late as 1914.

Le Vieux Carré (The French Quarter)

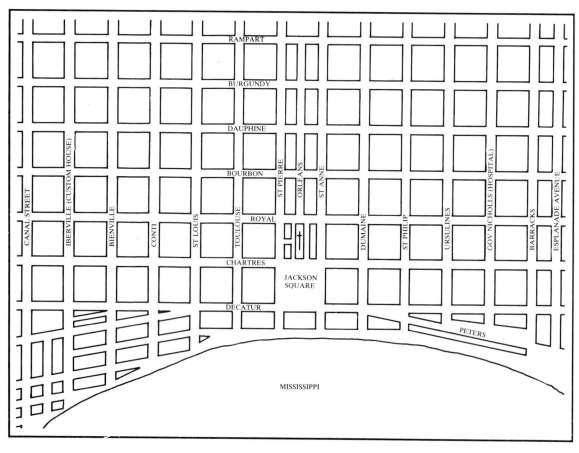

Bunk claimed that when he played at Dago Tony's and Pete Lala's the young Louis Armstrong used to sneak in and try to play his cornet. Bunk said that he taught him to play the blues and *Ballin' the Jack* and that he became quite proficient for his age; also that Louis used to follow him on parade to pick up his style. The standard story is that Armstrong learnt to play the cornet at the New Orleans Waifs Home, having been sent there for six months for firing a pistol during the 1913 New Year celebrations. Peter Davis, an assistant at the home, ran a brass band with help from Joe Howard, a schooled cornettist who played with Henry Allen's Brass Band in Algiers, and these men would certainly have been the first to teach Louis how to read music. Bunk, endorsed by Sidney Bechet, said that Louis could already play a bit before he went into the home though he was anxious to keep his family from knowing of this dubious accomplishment and of his association with musicians like Bunk.

Although Armstrong, when originally interviewed by enthusiasts, seems to have been happy to acknowledge that he learned from Bunk, in later years he denied it, crediting Joe Oliver as his only significant influence. However, in an interview with Fred Robbins, (on being asked about trying out on Bunk's horn) he said, 'Yeah, that was the ol' Eagle Hall down in New Orleans where the Bunk Johnson orchestra usta play . . . an' it was a pleasure to slip in there an' hear Bunk an' King Oliver an' the boys in the good ol' days.' Elsewhere he said of Bunk: 'How I used to follow him around. He could play funeral marches that made me cry.' Armstrong remembered the Eagle personnel already quoted, but with Bill (Willie Eli, son of James) Humphrey on clarinet in place of Bechet.

Bechet said that Bunk was the first to make him acquainted with Louis Armstrong, taking him to hear an adolescent vocal quartet in which Louis sang tenor. He recalled that when he was playing at 'Buddy Bartelot's place' with Bunk, the drummer, a notoriously informal character called Black Benny, took him to hear Armstrong and that he was astonished at how his proficiency had increased during his stay in the Waifs Home. Pops Foster recalled that Louis said that he had no regular job at this time but played Saturday nights at 'Buddy Bartletts tonk', evidently a saloon run by Bolden's former Master of Ceremonies, Buddy Bartley, who used to do balloon and parachute stunts at Lincoln Park. Armstrong was no doubt called in to take Bunk's place so that he could play for the Eagles for their important Saturday job.

The truth regarding the relationship between Bunk Johnson and Louis Armstrong is whatever one wants it to be. Certainly Bunk was not a formal 'professor' like James Humphrey, who gave so many players in and around New Orleans the foundations of a musical career. But the evidence of the young Louis having at least listened very hard to the older man at a formative stage, and benefitted from some simple tuition on his cornet, seems pretty clear, and it is to some extent corroborated by the structure of his playing. This is not to deny the later, and probably greater, influence of Joe Oliver. It does seem, however, that eventually Armstrong became fed up with all the enthusiasts who asked him about Bunk, and also with Bunk's remarks about his ungratefulness, and that this led to his denials of owing anything, apart from some influence on his tone, to his early hero.

Bunk claimed to have taught many of the younger generation of New Orleans cornet players. With his egotistical view of his own importance, we must beware of reading too much into this, and it may be that a few passing remarks of advice or encouragement would have been enough for Bunk to consider the recipient his debtor for life. Yet is does seem that for a brief period Bunk was the one who showed the up-and-coming players that, with the musical devices he had learnt from Professor Cutchey and, probably, from the Creole cornettists, Bolden's crude innovations of sound and rhthym could be directed along a more subtle path. Bunk may well have been the first to introduce minor and diminished chords in 'hot' music, using them to provide variation in the otherwise monotonous cornet lead. He further varied this monotony by shifts in the timing of phrases.

Bunk's recollection of playing at Tom Anderson's dance hall in Storyville may reasonably be relocated among the odd jobs which he did during his period with the Eagle Band. During his time in New Orleans he is said to have played in a number of other brass bands, including the Excelsior, the Diamond Stone and the Melrose in New Orleans and the Algiers Pacific and Henry Allen's Brass Band from across the river. The truth is probably that the uptown brass bands were fluid in personnel, recruiting extras by the job to supplement a hard core of regulars. A musician who wanted to work and was known to be capable of playing would have had no difficulty in getting onto one parade after another, without any particular personal allegiance. Recruitment by that severely formal Creole institution, the Excelsior Brass Band, must, however, be accounted a compliment to his musicianship and discipline, as must the occasional call to play in John Robichaux' orchestra.

Other musicians' memories of Bunk Johnson in New Orleans from these years are usually full of praise for his playing, particularly of the blues. It was his tone and the smooth flow of his invention that made the most impact on all who heard him. But if, as he claimed, he was the leader of cornet style in New Orleans it can have been only for a brief period. At the time he disappeared

Tom Anderson's Arlington Annex was at 201 North Basin St. at Iberville St. from 1901-c 1925; Anderson's Cafe was at 110-12 North Rampart St. c 1900-c 1912, then Tom Anderson's New Cabaret and Restaurant took over, at 122-6 North Rampart St., c 1912

from the city there was a general feeling that he was 'burned out'. The music was becoming more competitive, with bright young men of great power and exciting impact arriving on the scene and established musicians such as Joe Oliver and Freddie Keppard achieving their full potential. The last word on his status comes from another highly rated blues cornettist, Thomas 'Mutt' Carey: 'He had marvellous ideas and I used to like to hear him play. He wasn't quite the drive man that Joe and Freddie were, however, he always stayed behind the beat instead of getting out there in the lead like those other men. Bunk was good, and he was solid when he was playing. Bunk had plenty of competition on his way up and he never was the king down there.'

CHAPTER 2

NEW ORLEANS CONTEMPORARIES

New Orleans, during Bunk Johnson's heyday, was at a musical cross-roads. The established arbiters of style, the Creoles, were finding their credo of sound, legitimate musicianship and dedication to the printed notes challenged by upstart, uneducated men who could use their very crudeness of approach as an advantage. Bolden may have been the first of these, and he was not lacking in followers of a later generation; some among the Creoles even realised the advantages of his free, exciting style in attracting popular attention; they probably also found in it a release from the constraints of Creole education and a means of imposing their personalities on the music. Bunk was probably one of the earliest to suggest a middle way, showing that musical refinements and a disciplined approach could be applied to this new freedom without negating its vitality and colourfulness. In the meantime the two streams, straight Creole 'downtown' style and black 'uptown' experimentation, continued in parallel, but not without a good deal of cross-fertilisation.

Manuel Perez, who was already active during Bolden's reign, epitomises the Creole technique of cornet playing. Although remembered by Big Eye Nelson and Alphonse Picou (Creole clarinettists who were not averse to mixing with the rougher element) as the first cornettist to play jazz in New Orelans, Perez was a trained musician. He is said to have been the finest brass-band exponent in the city before he ventured into the saloons with his Imperial Orchestra in 1900, and he was such a strong player that he provided a good deal of excitement, even though he played from written arrangements.

Perez' style, which influenced a later generation of Creoles, may, as it evolved, have taken on some of the colour of the 'ratty' (self-taught, crude) musicians, including a more flexible use of mutes and a more urgent rhythm. As the star performer of the Onward

Brass Band, he brought on younger men who played beside him, including some, such as Joe Oliver, who were moving along lines suggested by Bolden. There is nothing to show that he held these less constrained musicians in contempt, and he may even have learned from them. In later years he was happy to employ an improvising trumpet player to liven up the sound of the Imperial, but in Bunk's time the orchestra would have depended upon Perez alone for the cornet part.

Of all those who followed Bolden's line, the rattiest was Freddie Keppard. Born in 1889 or 1890, the son of a musician, he played mandolin, guitar and accordion before receiving cornet tuition from Adolphe Alexander of the Onward Brass Band. In 1906 and 1907 Keppard organised his Olympia Orchestra with his brother Louis on guitar. Initially working in the downtown halls, it seems to have been a relatively straight group, with Freddie a capable musician as well as an exciting one. He had a beautiful big tone and put a lot of feeling into his playing, and he also commanded a range of trick effects, such as growling and neighing like a horse. When he widened his area of operation to play at the uptown saloons (and no doubt adjusted his style to suit), he captured the public imagination and received the honorary title of 'King', which had been vacant since Bolden's committal.

Freddie Keppard is said to have played with the Eagle Band at times between 1907 and 1910; he also worked in various Storyville clubs as well as keeping the Olympia going. When, in 1914, the bass player Bill Johnson needed a group from his home town to work in Los Angeles, he sent for Keppard, who took several of his musicians with him to form the Original Creole Orchestra. They toured on the Orpheum theatre circuit, and made visits to New York and Chicago, where Keppard settled and worked for, among others, the well-known bandleaders Erskine Tate and Charles 'Doc' Cooke. He recorded several times between 1912 and 1926; his style, though squarely based on ragtime, is extremely forceful and dynamic, giving some idea of the power he could exercise, with relatively simple musical means, in the flesh.

When Keppard left New Orleans the Olympia banner was taken up by the Creole violinist Armand J. Piron, and the cornettist he chose was Joe Oliver. However, Oliver seemed already to have taken Keppard's honorary crown from him; he had waited for this satisfaction for some time, for he was a slow developer. Born in 1885, most of his early work was as an irregular in brass bands the Melrose, the Onward, Henry Allen's and the Eagle. He also played occasionally with the Eagle dance band before Bunk joined it and sat in for Bunk in the Original Superior Orchestra. He was with the Magnolia Band, formed by Louis Keppard, around 1908. The band's bass player, Pops Foster, said that they took him on because he had a book full of engagements lined up; none of these materialised, but the band was successful, playing in Storyville at Huntz and Nagel's dance hall, close by Billy Phillips's 101 Ranch, where Keppard was in residence, and Rice's, where Perez was playing.

Joe Oliver came into his own while he was working in Richard M. Jones's Four Hot Hounds at the Abadie Cabaret. Keppard, across the street at Pete Lala's, was attracting all the attention, so Oliver went out onto the sidewalk and blew, as Jones said, 'the most beautiful stuff I have ever heard'. After that the place filled up and Joe said, 'Now that ***** won't bother me no more!' Oliver had no trouble drawing a crowd thereafter and had the pick of the dance-hall jobs. He worked in Kid Ory's band with Johnny Dodds on clarinet, at Pete Lala's in 1914. Ory claimed that he was the first to publicise the cornettist as 'King' Oliver, the name by which he was subsequently best known, and that he helped to refine his loud, rough style. Oliver left New Orleans, again at the instigation of Bill Johnson, to work at the Royal Gardens in Chicago in 1918. Johnson's first choice was the emergent Buddy Petit, but the latter refused to leave home.

Ory's band had been one of the best in the city since the time he had arrived from Laplace around 1912. Oliver's predecessor in the band was Mutt Carey, who joined after working in the Crescent Orchestra led by his brother Jack. Jack Carey was not a powerful trombonist, but he was a good musician and is credited with developing the New Orleans standard *Tiger Rag* from a quadrille, imitating the tiger's roar with his slide. However, in his brother's estimation, he could not compete with Ory, either as a trombonist or as a leader, and there seems to have been some jealousy when Mutt moved on. Bunk Johnson played with Jack Carey, mainly on out-of-town excursions, around 1913.

Mutt Carey was considered second only to Joe Oiver as an expert in the imaginative use of mutes of all kinds. He left New Orleans before Oliver in Billy and Mary Mack's touring show, which also included Johnny Dodds. After arriving in Chicago, Mutt joined a band led by Lawrence Duhé, a clarinettist who had also worked for Ory before going north with a complete New Orleans group. Mutt stepped in when Duhé's cornettist, Sugar Johnny Smith, died of pneumonia, but soon returned home and asked Oliver to take his place. Thus, when he left for Chicago, Joe had two jobs lined up. He played with both bands for a while and then took over the leadership of Duhé's group, replacing the clarinettist with Johnny Dodds around 1920.

When Oliver left New Orleans he was replaced in Kid Ory's band by Louis Armstrong who, since leaving the Waifs Home, had been very much under 'Papa Joe's' wing; he had learned from him

The SS JS

so well that he fitted in immediately and soon became the sensation of the city (although the title of 'King' seemed to have gone to Chicago permanently with Oliver). Armstrong spent two years in riverboat bands led by Fate Marable, sailing between St Louis and New Orleans alongside his former instructor Joe Howard and a fine multi-instumentalist and teacher, Davey Jones from Lutcher. In 1922 Oliver sent for him to join his Creole Jazz Band in Chicago, and the results were captured in a most distinguished series of recordings during 1923; Oliver leads with great drive and proves his expertise with mutes, and Armstrong complements him perfectly with a lyrical part that in places seems to show a definite debt to Bunk.

Ory moved to California for the good of his health in 1919, although he later rejoined his former sideman King Oliver in Chicago. Mutt Carey followed Ory west and recorded in his band in 1922, showing some Keppard-like tendencies grafted onto a basically schooled approach. This was the first black New Orleans group to have its recordings issued, under the name of a local enterpreneur as Spikes' Seven Pods of Pepper. Another cornettist who moved to California was Ernest 'Nenny' Coycault, who had replaced Bunk Johnson in the Original Superior Orchestra. He made a number of recordings with Sonny Clay's Plantation Orchestra in Los Angeles from 1923, in which he showed the Creole attributes of accuracy and adherence to the beat enhanced by a bubbling vitality and flexible range of tone.

31

Oscar 'Papa' Celestin was a straight but powerful cornet player who worked with the trombonist William Ridgley in the Silver Leaf Orchestra; they played together at the 101 Ranch and the Tuxedo Dance Hall, where Celestin took over the leadership of the band in 1910. When in 1913, the dance hall's manager, Harry Parker, and Billy Phillips of the 101 Ranch shot each other, both establishments were closed down. Celestin never worked at the Tuxedo again, but he kept its name for his dance and brass bands. He always used accomplished musicians, although he himself was not a good reader, and his band became very popular at such resorts on Lake Pontchartrain as Spanish Fort, which catered for white society. Probably on account of this, his was one of the very few bands to be recorded in New Orleans during the 1920s. Papa Celestin was still playing in the 1940s; he received a good deal of publicity for his work on Bourbon Street, which maintained him as an attraction for the New Orleans tourists up to his death in 1954.

A cornettist who worked with Celestin, and also in the Silver Leaf Orchestra, was Hippolyte Charles. Charles, who had to give up playing in 1925 on account of a ruptured spleen, came to New Orleans from Parks, close to New Iberia. This was the area settled by the Acadians, French emigrants who found their original destination, Canada, inhospitable, and travelled down the length of North America to the swamp country west of New Orleans. As a result of the Acadians inter-breeding with the freed slaves, there evolved a subculture which was the bucolic equivalent of that enjoyed by the New Orleans 'Creoles of Colour'; it had its own 'Cajun' country music which persists to this day in the form of 'Zydeco'.

Buddy Petit, a later legend of New Orleans trumpet playing, told George Lewis that 'Bunk and Joe Johnson were the men who knocked me out.' Joe Johnson was said by both Louis Armstrong and Lee Collins to have had a style very similar to Petit's. It has also been alleged, though without any clear evidence, that Joe was Bunk's brother. Pops Foster knew him well, and most of what we know of Joe's career comes from the bass player, who was with him in the Rozelle band around 1907. He originally played guitar, then changed to cornet on which he became very proficient. He could make his cornet sound like a chicken, but generally 'he played the middle range and played it rough and beautiful.'

When the Rozelle Band broke up in 1908 Joe Johnson went to work in the Primrose Band, led by the trombonist Hamp Benson. This was a small reading group that worked in the Storyville cabarets and played on Sunday nights at the Come Clean Hall in Gretna, across the river. Joe also played occasional jobs with Pops Foster and the Dutrey brothers – Sam (clarinet) and Honoré (trombone) – and with Richard M. Jones. When, sometime between 1910 and 1912, Benson took the money owing to the Primrose Band and left New Orleans, Joe joined the Eagle Band, possibly in place of Bunk. Pops reckoned that working with the Eagles was the death of Joe, a church-going man, as he could not adapt to the heavy drinking that was an essential part of their lifestyle. He was already sick with tuberculosis when he left them to play with Jack Carey's Crescent Orchestra, and he died, according to Pops, around 1914.

CHAPTER 3

ANNEES DE PELERINAGE

It is not possible to pin down the exact date of Bunk Johnson's departure from New Orleans; in fact he may have returned there sporadically to play with the Eagles and others. His movements are impossible to document precisely, and it is necessary to rely on fragmentary reports in order to build up any picture of his life. Around 1914 Bunk made a trip to Alexandria, some 200 miles to the north-west, with the pianist Clarence Williams and the celebrated itinerant trombonist Zue Robertson, whom Bunk rated very highly. Zue had worked with Bolden's drummer Cornelius Tillman in New Orleans and then left to join the Kit Carson Wild West Show. After returning home he played with Manuel Perez, John Robichaux and Richard M. Jones before settling in Chicago to work with Jelly Roll Morton and King Oliver.

Clarence Williams came from Plaquemine and played piano as a boy in local events, but when he ran away from home with Billy Kersand's minstrel show it was as a singer and master of ceremonies. In New Orleans he applied himself to his piano studies to a point where, in 1913, at the age of 15 he was able to get a job in one of the classier Storyville bordellos. Later he teamed up with Armand J. Piron in a music publishing business and both men moved to New York but they fell out and Piron returned to New Orleans while Williams continued his successful entrepreneurial career in the North. His New York recordings during the 1920s often featured such well-known New Orleans musicians as King Oliver, Louis Armstrong and Sidney Bechet.

Bunk's Alexandria job was in a sporting house, and the three men teamed up with the notorious 'Pensacola Kid', Paul Wyer, on violin. Wyer was a talented musician who played piano, clarinet and violin, but he preferred gambling (he many times confronted Jelly Roll Morton across the pool table) and only made music when he needed the money; his composition *Keep a-Knockin'* was the

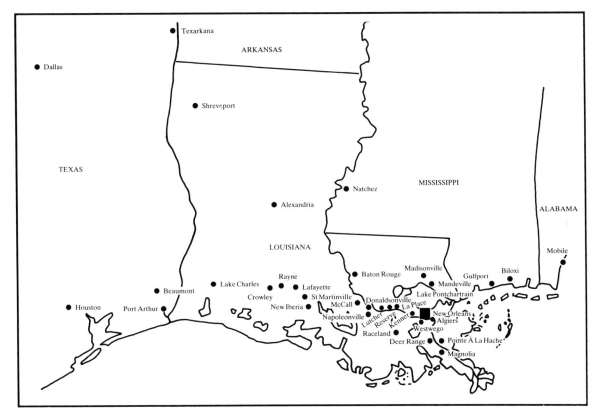

Louisiana

original for the New Orleans standard *Bucket's got a hole in it*. Williams recalled that the Alexandria venue had a player-piano that was hard to play manually, so the musicians moved to the house next door, which had an easier piano and also offered better pay. This caused trouble with their previous landlady, who had police connections, and they had to leave Alexandria after only a short stay.

Bunk is said to have made some trips with Jack Carey's band around the end of his time in New Orleans. The group visited the small towns to the west, including New Iberia, where Bunk was a great success playing *Casey Jones*; this may have helped him decide to make his home there. Some commentators assume that he went straight to New Iberia when he left his home city, but he was also to be found in Mandeville, across Lake Pontchartrain from New Orleans. Bunk said that he taught Tommy Ladnier, a cornet player who later found some fame in the North: 'I taught Tommy. First piece I taught Tommy to play was *Big Chief Battle Axe*. And Tommy turned out to be real good.' He also said, 'Tommy Ladnier – well, he's from Mandeville, Louisiana. I was teaching school over there about four years, and Tommy learned with me over there.' Ladnier was born in nearby Florenceville in 1900, and left for Chicago around 1917. George Lewis, who lived in Mandeville

35

during his teens, remembered hearing him in the Independence Band led by the clarinettist Isidore Fritz, a fine musician who preferred to stay on his own patch rather than to chance his luck in New Orleans. George said that Bunk would appear in Mandeville from time to time to train the band or play an engagement with the musicians. Lewis was not playing professionally at that time, but he would sometimes sit in with them, and he credited Fritz with some influence on his playing.

Others who admired Bunk when he was in Mandeville were the trumpeters Ernie Cagnolatti and Andy Anderson. Cagnolatti, who lived in the adjacent town of Madisonville from his birth in 1911 until he moved to New Orleans in 1919, must have heard Bunk towards the end of his time there for his playing to have made any significant impression. Ernie's brother Clabere was the Independence Band's drummer, and the group used to rehearse at the Cagnolattis' house.

Another young cornet player whom Bunk claimed to have influenced played occasionally with the Independence Band. This was Buddy Petit, remembered by George Lewis, who often played with him, as the best trumpeter he ever heard. His original inspiration was probably Manuel Perez, but Lewis and others, including Lee Collins, have said that Petit's playing was very similar to Bunk's. Collins's own style was close to Bunk's in those days, and Punch Miller, another who remarked on the similarity, was in turn influenced by Petit. If anyone took over the mantle of 'King' in New Orleans in the days after Oliver and Armstrong had left the city, it was Buddy Petit. He played in the Eagle Band at some time after Bunk left it, and went to California with Frankie Dusen on an ill-founded and short-lived trip to join Jelly Roll Morton in 1917. From his return until the mid-1920s his band, despite various changes of personnel, more or less ruled the roost in New Orleans. He too was a heavy drinker and eventually, like Bolden, became unreliable in his habits; but Lewis recalled him as being able to play quite well right up to the time of his death in 1931.

During the period between 1914 and 1918 Bunk Johnson is said to have played at the Colonial Hotel in Bogalousa, to the north; in the capital of Louisiana, Baton Rouge, up the Mississippi, with his old drummer colleague Walter Brundy; and at Lake Charles to the west, within striking distance of New Iberia. At the end of this time he probably spent a few years touring with circuses and minstrel shows. He claimed to have worked in P. G. Loral's Circus, Holcamp's Georgia Smart Set, McCabe's Minstrels and Hagenbeck and Wallace's Circus. In Bunk's recollections all these activities took place during the first decade of the century. However, one Willie, Bill or W. Johnson turns up as a cornettist in

36

press references to Baker's Concert Band of Nitro, West Virginia, in 1918. This band was led by P. G. Lowery, a well-known show band director and cornet virtuoso. Zue Robertson also worked in Lowery's band, but probably a year or so earlier.

Another positive sighting of Bunk Johnson occurred in 1922. He was the leader of the band in one of the Greater Holcamp Carnival Shows, which was touring Texas. The proprietor of this particular show was the father of Al Rose, the well-known New Orleans jazz historian who in his time produced many concerts and radio and television shows featuring his revered musician friends. At that time Rose was only six years old, but he was already able to respond to the colour of the Wild West parade, the minstrel show and, particularly, the band. The cornettist, who occasionally looked after the boy when his parents were busy, was known to him as Willie. Much later, in New York, Bunk Johnson appeared in one of Rose's concerts, and he immediately recognised him as that same 'Willie'. Bunk recalled that Albert Nicholas, also at the concert, had been the Holcamp clarinettist and that Baby Dodds had been the drummer. He also remembered a one-legged blues singer in the show who had later become quite successful; on investigation this turned out to be Furry Lewis, who confirmed Bunk's story.

The gaps in documentation of Bunk Johnson's movements between 1914 and 1930 are such that his various other touring jobs may have occurred at any time during the period, as may his claimed visits to Chicago, Montana and San Francisco. New Iberia does, however, seem to have been his base during the 1920s, to the extent that he bought himself a house and married a local girl, Maude Fontenette, the daughter of the town's principal negro bandleader. Maude was apparently his second wife, but he seems never to have provided any details of his previous marriage. New Iberia was not a place where the Blacks were treated well, but this may have fostered a sense of community in them. Gustave Fontenette, a barber, founded the Banner Band around 1908 and it soon became popular, securing all the top jobs with both black and white customers. Gus himself was a very strong trombonist; Hippolyte Potier and George 'Pops' Hamilton played cornet, and another of Fontenette's daughters, Mercedes, played piano. Frankie Dusen's wife Lila, a professional pianist who toured with minstrel shows, was Gus Fontenette's aunt, and this connection with his previous New Orleans associations may have helped Bunk to become familiar with New Iberia.

Gus Fontenette was remembered by Hippolyte Charles, who came from the same area of Louisiana and retired there in his old age, as 'a serious businessman and a real good musician', capable of playing many instruments. Charles and Hippolyte Potier played together in a band in their home village of Parks, near St Martinville, before Charles went to New Orleans. The Banner Band was probably a country equivalent of John Robichaux's orchestra, but it evidently played in a forthright style: Potier's son Harold said that not many cornet players other than his father could match the loud sounds made by Gus Fontenette and his clarinet player, Jimmy Adam. Another who could, when he came on the scene, was Bunk Johnson. During Bunk's association with the band its personnel varied somewhat. Among those who worked for Fontenette were Jimmy Adam's brother Beauregard on violin, trumpet and saxophone, Bob Thomas on trombone, Ed Redium on banjo and violin, John Saunders on bass and Abbie 'Chinee' Foster on drums. Lawrence Duhé, who left Chicago in disgust when King Oliver took over his band at the Deluxe Café in 1919, settled in nearby Lafayette and often played with the Banner. So did the trumpeter Evan Thomas, the leader of the Black Eagle Band of Crowley, the band in which Duhé played regularly.

The Banner Band played not only in New Iberia; it had a regular territory that extended westwards into Texas, and it often worked in Beaumont, just over the border. The band never played in New Orleans, but was content to maintain its reputation as the best organisation in Louisiana outside the city. In addition to excursions with the New Iberia musicians, Bunk made trips as a soloist. On one occasion he was reported to be in the band at the American Theatre in Houston, Texas, and, on another, on tour with Dee Johnson's orchestra. The trumpeter Oran 'Hot Lips' Page, who was born in Dallas, recalled carrying Bunk's baggage from the station when he arrived there at one time. Bunk was also said to have played the saxophone proficiently, and he certainly knew enough to teach the young Teddy Johnson, who was just starting out on the instrument and had joined a band from New Orleans that was playing in Port Arthur, Texas, how to play *Ain't she sweet*. This was while he was on a trip with the Banner Band.

During the 1920s Bunk also seems to have played quite regularly with the Black Eagles. Evan Thomas is remembered by all who heard him as a tremendous trumpet player, particularly powerful in the upper register. There is some doubt whether he was a trained musician, but he had an iron lip and a very adequate technique. He found the perfect foil in Bunk, who preferred to play what he called the second trumpet part, providing lyrical subtleties to complement his partner's exuberant drive. Duhé and Abbie Foster were regular members of the band, and the trombonists were all well-known New Orleans musicians – Bob Thomas, Joe 'Kid' Avery and Harrison Brazlee.

Harold Potier and his wife Mercedes (née Fontenette)

remembered Bunk as a very musical, sweet (meaning lyrical) trumpet player who could stand up and perform with any band. He was a great talker, and very enjoyable to listen to; he drank a lot, but this did not make him difficult to get along with. Bunk and Evan Thomas used to get into long arguments about music and, if they couldn't resolve them, they would go and see Professor Oger, a resident of Crowley who had been trained in Europe and played in a symphony orchestra in Paris. Oger had the best reading band in the area, probably of the concert variety. Morris Dauphine, who returned to New Iberia after playing saxophone with Celestin's Tuxedo Band in New Orleans, said that Bunk's style was more advanced than that of the local musicians and that he could play any kind of music but that he could not beat Evan Thomas at playing the blues.

A saxophonist who played with the Black Eagles in the late 1920s, Baker Millian, remembered Bunk, Thomas and Professor Oger playing trumpet trios. Millian was born in Crowley in 1908; he first played with the local Yelpin' Hounds and then, for a short time, with Chris Kelly in New Orleans. On his return to Crowley he worked with the Black Eagles until they disbanded in 1929. The two trumpeters continued their partnership in the Banner Band, but a year or so later Bunk was in Lake Charles, playing with Millian in the Imperial Band. The pianist was a local girl, Nellie Lutcher, aged 15, and her father, Isaac 'Skinner' Lutcher, played string bass in the band. Nellie Lutcher later became famous on the West Coast as a cabaret singer and recording artist, accompanying herself on piano.

Harold Potier, who started playing trumpet with the Banner Band towards the end of the 1920s, remembered that Bunk Johnson was always receiving letters from King Oliver. Oliver's great days were over and he was reduced to touring the South, and he had trouble getting the musicians he wanted. One such letter found Bunk in Eltra, Texas, where he had remained after touring with Dee Johnson and was working as a handyman in a funeral parlour, apparently not playing at all. This letter, which was printed in *Jazzmen*, was said to have been written in early 1930. It has always intrigued record collectors, because Oliver wrote that he had just made a recording with Lizzie Miles, a singer from New Orleans. Joe did record with Lizzie in New York, in June 1928, and although she did have a session on 27th February 1930, there is no trumpet on it. It has been suggested that Oliver may have been a visitor to the studio on that occasion; he may even have played on one title, *Too Slow Blues*, which was never issued. Not having seen the original letter, I do not know if it was dated by Oliver; if not it may actually have been written earlier and therefore have referred to the session of June 1928. In view of Bunk's obscure situation at the time, it may have taken a long time to find him.

Oliver's letter chided Bunk for not taking up 'two good jobs' that his friend had lined up for him, and said that the writer would look for other opportunities. Bunk may actually have travelled to Kansas City to meet Oliver in response to another letter. Oliver played one dance there in June 1930 and then moved on to Wichita for a few days. Bunk turned up in Kansas City shortly afterwards and worked with the Texas pianist Sammy Price at the Yellow Front Café. Whether he intended to join Oliver there or not, he does not seem to have made contact. It is not clear whether this was his only visit, or how long he stayed, but it was from Kansas City that George Lewis remembered him arriving in Crowley by freight train late in 1931. It seemed a timely appearance, for Evan Thomas was getting his band together again for a tour of the South-west and Mexico.

Thomas had recruited Lewis in New Orleans, having known him from the time when he had visited Crowley in Chris Kelly's band. Lewis, though reluctant to travel, was not finding work easy to get in the city. Bunk's expertise was useful in helping the band to prepare; along with their traditional material, they wanted to play the latest tunes of the day, such as *Stardust* and *You rascal, you*. Although he was happy to play with them, Bunk would not live with the rest of the band. Harold Potier was asked to join the group on saxophone, but he declined and remembered that they took a man called Al Wilson instead. 'Big Eye' Louis Robertson was on piano, Walter Preston played banjo and Chinee Foster was on drums.

Before the tour proper began, a dance was arranged in the nearby small town of Rayne. There was a large crowd present, for the Black Eagles were a popular attraction and had been out of action for two years. Before the dance some members of the band bought a good deal of dubious liquor from a bootlegger called John Guillory in a shed behind the hall, but Evan Thomas was not among them. Guillory, who had been in the penitentiary, asked after Thomas. Somebody said, apparently without jutification, that the trumpet player had been fooling around with Guillory's wife while he as inside. Some time after the dance started Guillory came into the hall and asked Evan to play *I'll be glad when you're dead, you rascal, you*; Thomas knew what was going on, but according to custom he had to play the tune. At the end of the number Guillory came up on the stand and attacked the trumpeter with a knife. Thomas was stabbed in the back, but apparently managed to stagger some distance before he collapsed and died.

Most of the band's instruments were damaged in the fracas although Lewis managed to escape with his clarinet. He said that Bunk was able to salvage only his mouthpiece from the wreckage, while Bunk himself claimed that both his instrument and his heart for music had been destroyed by the tragedy. At the same time his teeth were evidently giving him some trouble. Harold Potier recalled that, when he was playing with the Banner Band, Bunk had two front teeth missing; he would tie a piece of string into the gap, to support his lip, and play as well as ever. He did continue to perform, probably using a borrowed trumpet, for a while after the murder. Nellie Lutcher remembered working with him in a band led by the New Orleans reed player Paul 'Polo' Barnes which toured Louisiana in 1932 and 1933. Barnes (who had earlier worked with Oscar Celestin) left King Oliver's band, fed up with innumerable one-night stands, at the end of 1931, although he did go back to him later. After this Bunk's wanderings seem to have come to an end, and his musical activities were reduced to some occasional local work with the Banner Band, in which he may have played tuba more often than trumpet.

CHAPTER 4

LIFE GOES ON

While Bunk Johnson was in obscurity, rambling from one small town to another or vegetating in New Iberia, New Orleans jazz went through its most important period of development, leading up to the time when it left its purely regional characteristics far behind. King Oliver, Jelly Roll Morton and, particularly, Louis Armstrong played an important part in this evolution, which was understandably given its dynamic by the greater sophistication of of audiences in the northern cities and by the growth of the media of communication – the radio and the gramophone.

In Chicago King Oliver and Morton led successful bands which grew larger to meet the demands of the time for a smoother sort of music. Both men, with very mixed results, ventured to New York in the search for continuing fame and fortune, and by the end of the 1920s both found themselves overtaken by the innovations of the younger men – Armstrong and Henry 'Red' Allen, son of the brass band leader from Algiers, foremost among them. Bands became bigger and more organised, and the ability of musicians to read music fluently was once again valuable. Red Allen found his forte in the Luis Russell orchestra, which took over where King Oliver left off, and used some of his former sidemen; it was a band in which a big sound was achieved without the New Orleans colour and rhythm being jettisoned. Louis Armstrong's trumpet playing became such a hot property that a large orchestra was built up merely to act as a backdrop for him, emphasising his great talent for showmanship.

Some other New Orleans trumpet players found it harder to give up the habits of their home town. Lee Collins developed his style into one of extreme expressive excitement, but when he was asked to substitute for Allen in Russell's band he found his inability to read an insuperable hurdle; he ended his days finding what work he could in the rough Chicago clubs. Tommy Ladnier, whose expressed desire was to sound exactly like King Oliver and who played second trumpet in his idol's band for a while, found some success, and the benefits of European travel, in the orchestras of Sam Wooding, Fletcher Henderson and Noble Sissle. He teamed up with his friend Sidney Bechet during the early 1930s but was unable to find work to suit his temperament. He disappeared into the backwoods, where he remained until Hugues Panassié sought him out to take part in his revivalist recording activities in 1938; it was a short-lived, though welcome, revival on Ladnier's part, for he died shortly afterwards.

Punch Miller, who was inspired to play the cornet when Bunk Johnson played at his home town of Raceland, west of New Orleans, before World War I, was something of a wanderer. Like Mutt Carey, he left New Orleans with Billy and Mary Mack and was very popular in the Chicago clubs during the late 1920s. He spent the best part of the 1930s playing in circuses, and his life continued in this peripatetic vein until he returned to New Orleans, a sick man, in 1956. After his recovery he took part in a good deal of recording sessions with George Lewis and others, showing that much of his athletic, individual style was still intact.

Punch Miller had a successful band in New Orleans in the early 1920s, and the cornettists he vied with were Buddy Petit, Chris Kelly and Henry 'Kid' Rena (pronounced René). George Lewis played with all three and accounted Petit, a rough, informal character, as the greatest. Petit was a fierce and expressive performer who made his musical points without using the higher register of his instrument; he was unbeatable in a cutting contest or band battle before drink took its toll. Rena, on the other hand, produced effortless high-range improvisations but did not have the nerve for extended competitions. Neither could compete, where playing the blues was concerned, with Chris Kelly, the most popular musician in New Orleans with the rougher element. Kelly, blowing quietly, muted, but with the utmost intensity, could turn *Careless Love* into an orgiastic experience – to the extent that some renamed it *Kelly's Love*.

Chris Kelly would take on several jobs at once, and therefore trained some of the younger musicians to play in his style. Renditions of *Careless Love* by his followers Avery 'Kid' Howard and Joseph 'De De' Pierce go some way to demonstrate the hypnotic power that Kelly could exercise. Buddy Petit's style can be realised only in a more roundabout way by an analysis of the common elements in the playing of men who admitted his influence – Lee Collins, Punch Miller, Guy Kelly and Herb Morand. The recordings made in Chicago by these musicians during the 1930s show the deep, intense tone and dynamically angular approach to rhythm they had in common, as well as many of their own

individual characteristics. Kid Rena, when recorded in 1940, was a *Lee Collins*
shadow of his former self, and his reputation rests entirely on those
who remembered him with respect and admiration.

Although New Orleans lagged behind the North in its attitude to
music, an innate conservatism maintaining the status quo there for
longer than was tolerated in the sophisticated cities of Chicago and
New York, it did follow the musical trends of the 1920s and 1930s.
The availability of recordings by Louis Armstrong and Red Allen
gave cornet players the ambition to explore more fully the
capabilities of their instruments, and saxophones were welcomed
for the fuller, sweeter sound that they gave to a band, even to the
extent where a recognisable New Orleans saxophone style
developed. Big bands led by such musicians as Joe Robichaux
(nephew of John), Sidney Desvigne and Paul Barnes played

arrangements that aped those to be heard on radio and recordings. At the same time the homely, social aspect of music-making continued, as part-time musicians played in the modest dance halls or on the streets to supplement their labourer's earnings.

One development that took place, in New Orleans as elsewhere, was the general replacement in jazz of the cornet by the trumpet. Although the instruments are similar to play, the cornet's conical bore gives it a warm, dark tone, full of harmonics, while the straight trumpet sounds bright, clean and loud. The cornet was probably more suited to the ensemble characteristics of early jazz, and was easier to play so long as the players stayed in the middle range, but as jazzmen became more adventurous the trumpet was found to be more impressive as a solo instrument. However, it is often difficult to tell, particularly on early recordings, which instrument is in use.

Louis Armstrong played the cornet until around 1926, when he changed to the trumpet, and many of his contemporaries seem to have done the same. In the conservative and less affluent milieu of New Orleans, the change probably took place a little later, and perhaps in response to the success of Armstrong's recordings. Ironically, owing to his already fully formed style, his self-centredness and his itinerant lifestyle, one of the very few jazz trumpet players who seems to have been immune to Louis's influence was Bunk Johnson himself. It is not clear whether Bunk made the change to trumpet deliberately at any stage in his career. He was given one on his comeback, but he played it in a manner suited to the cornet, and it is doubtful whether he made any adjustment to his established style in order to take advantage of its enhanced capabilities. It is probable that his choice of instrument, like that of other New Orleans musicians, was more historical than musical.

CHAPTER 5

A NEW SET OF TEETH

From 1932 Bunk Johnson lived in New Iberia, making no impact on the world of jazz. His music-making was limited to teaching the local children under the WPA education programme and occasionally appearing as a whistler at local carnivals. His teeth and his spirit were broken, yet he seems to have kept the respect of the local musicians. He worked as a truck driver for the Konniko Rice Mill and also as a labourer. The harshness of his life was softened by an intriguing benefactor, Weeks Hall, the owner of a mansion on the banks of the nearby Bayou Tesche called The Shadows. Hall was an artist, an eccentric and a recluse; he did not suffer fools gladly or welcome intrusions into his idyllic privacy, but, perhaps on account of his hatred of racial prejudice, he seems to have had a soft spot for the local negro musicians. Until Bunk came along, however, it does not appear that he paid much attention to their music. Bunk stood out among them as a man of intelligence and an irrepressible talker; he was also an ideal subject for Hall's benevolence – a tireless consumer of free meals, drinks and tobacco and a truly independent spirit who did not embarrass his benefactor with any overt show of gratitude. Bunk probably did odd jobs around the house and garden, but much of his time was spent fishing in the bayou at the back of the house. Whether or not he was resigned to the fact that his musical career was apparently over, there is no way that Bunk can have foreseen, even in his wildest dreams, what the future held for him.

In 1938 Frederic Ramsey Jr, having graduated from Princeton, joined the publishing firm of Harcourt, Brace. Being a jazz enthusiast, he felt that a properly researched and written book on the subject was needed. When his employers agreed, he and another enthusiast, Charles Edward Smith, teamed up as editors. They enlisted the help of others who were sympathetic, notably a man who was establishing a reputation as an indefatigable collector of early jazz records. Bill Russell, whose particular interest at that time was the boogie-woogie piano style, interviewed many of the musicians who were playing in Chicago and New York. Naturally, a number of these hailed from New Orleans, and several of them, including Sidney Bechet, Clarence Williams, Richard M. Jones, Lee Collins and Zutty Singleton, remembered a trumpet player called 'Bunk' – over whose surname they were by no means unanimous – as a fine early musician and an influence on Louis Armstrong. Discussion with Armstrong himself revealed that the latter had recently played at a dance in New Iberia where Bunk (whose name was Johnson) had been present; although unable to play trumpet, he had sung some scat with the band.

Before learning his surname, Russell and Ramsey had sent a letter to the postmaster at New Iberia, asking for it to be delivered to an old negro trumpet player called Bunk. It eventually found its addressee, and Bunk proved to be an articulate, if not particularly grammatical, correspondent. A further series of letters was exchanged; the enthusiasts were only after information to incorporate in their book, to be called *Jazzmen*, but Bunk was very keen to start playing again, if only he could get a trumpet and a set of false teeth. Intrigued, the *Jazzmen* team set about raising money. For 60 dollars Dr Leonard Bechet made Bunk a set of teeth (which he used only for playing because they hurt when he ate or drove the truck), and the members of the Lu Watters band in San Francisco, who were enthusiastically re-creating the old styles of jazz, raised 25 dollars, which he used to buy a trumpet and a cornet from a pawn shop.

After these developments Bunk Johnson was Heywood Broun's first choice for a trumpeter when he went to New Orleans to record in August 1940. Bunk declined, however, saying that he was too busy teaching; more likely, though, he was not yet satisfied with the progress of his rehabilitation. Early the next year Louis Armstrong again visited New Iberia with his big band, and Bunk was able to play with them. Favourable reports from Armstrong appeared in *Down Beat* magazine, but none of the *Jazzmen* team had actually heard Bunk play. Eventually in February 1942 John Reid, who worked for RCA, sent a portable disc recorder down to New Orleans and a young jazz enthusiast, Mary Karoley, took it to New Iberia. Bunk played some unaccompanied trumpet into it, including a rendition of *Maple Leaf Rag*, and also recorded an interview. He was apologetic about the sounds he made, saying that the trumpet he had was little better than a car horn or a coffee pot. He followed this up with an urgent request to Sidney Bechet and Louis Armstrong to send him a proper trumpet, and included some ingratiating remarks addressed to Bill Russell.

When Russell and Eugene Williams heard the recordings they

thought it would be worth making some professional ones, if only out of historical interest. While a student at Columbia, Williams had started a little magazine called *Jazz Information* with Ralph Gleason and Ralph de Toledano. (This was around 1939, the same time that *Jazzmen*, which included some colourful reminiscing by Bunk, was published; it seems that the book's first edition was a very limited one, as full publication was held up until after the war.) The magazine sprang out of the new vogue for collecting the early jazz records and analysing and theorising about their significance. It seems to have ceased publication by 1942, when Williams began looking for another outlet for his energy. He had started his own record label under the name, Jazz Information, reissuing limited editions of early material, and he wanted to record a live session featuring Bunk. He and Russell persuaded a young enthusiast who was also a trumpet player, Bill Rosenberg, to provide a nearly new Selmer instrument for Bunk to play.

As Williams and Russell were making their plans to go to New Orleans to record Bunk, so were three other men on the West Coast. Dave Stuart was the proprietor of the Jazz Man shop in Los Angeles, which issued records under the same name. With two others of like mind, Bill Colburn and Hal McIntyre, he headed for New Orleans, and the two parties met in New Iberia. They discussed the session with Bunk and decided that it would be best if the records were issued on the Jazz Man label, which had a wider distribution than Jazz Information. Russell had earlier canvassed Jimmie Noone in Chicago regarding the best clarinettist; Noone's recommendation was 'Big Eye' Louis Nelson, who had taken part in the Kid Rena session. Russell was not convinced that Nelson was forceful enough, but thought that Jim Robinson (also in that session) would be the ideal trombonist. Other musicians who seemed suitable, from their earlier reputations, were Johnny St Cyr, the banjoist on Louis Armstrong's Hot Five recordings, and Paul Barbarin, who had played drums with King Oliver and Red Allen.

The five men toured the New Orleans joints looking for musicians. Big Eye was found, playing quite well, but they thought his Creole style too soft. They wanted someone who performed after the manner of Johnny Dodds, the most intense clarinettist of all, who had died in Chicago two years previously. In searching for St Cyr, whom they failed to find, they were impressed by a bass player, Austin Young, who was the uncle of the famous tenor saxophonist Lester Young. There was no sign of Jim Robinson or of any clarinet player more suitable than Big Eye. But the next evening, when they went to hear Nelson again, they found that, although he was on the stand to make up the numbers, Nelson was too ill with ulcers to play much.

Jim Robinson

Bunk arrived in New Orleans by Greyhound bus on the next day. He had his trumpet in its case, and his spare clothes in a cardboard box tied up with string. At the bus station, and also when they called into a bar for a drink, all sorts of people recognised Bunk and stopped to talk to him. On being asked about possible clarinettists, he mentioned 'George', and an indistinct surname which they thought sounded like 'Strode' or 'Stewart'; he also considered that Alphonse Picou might be suitable because of his knowledge of the old ragtime numbers. Jim Robinson, when he was eventually contacted, told them that 'George's' name was Lewis, and that he lived on St Philip Street. Bunk confirmed that this was the man he had in mind, and they went to find him. Lewis had just returned from a job in Bunkie, Louisiana. He had a loose lower front tooth, which he wrapped with brown paper in order to play. His clarinet had rubber bands replacing the springs and various other ad hoc repairs, but he played it beautifully for them and it was agreed that he would take part in the session.

Paul Barbarin would not play with Bunk and the others because they were not union members, and nor would the cabaret entertainer and pianist Walter 'Fats' Pichon whom Bunk had suggested, to everyone's surprise. Walter Decou was chosen in his

49

place and an impromptu rehearsal of the group, still without banjo, bass or drums, was held at his house. All the listeners were impressed by the band's playing, and particularly by Bunk's drive and leadership. His choice of tunes was more ambitious than that of the others, and despite his patient tutoring there were several numbers that they could not get together at all. The traditional material went well, however, especially the blues. As they were packing up, Bunk sat down at Decou's piano and showed his prowess by rattling off a bit of *Maple Leaf Rag* and a composition by Tony Jackson, possibly to put Decou's rather homely musicianship in its place.

Austin Young said he would be glad to play in the session, but Johnny St Cyr was also afraid of union trouble. Bunk said that he did not want to have anything to do with union musicians, and promised to contact Ernest Rogers, who had impressed them when they heard Big Eye's band, and Willie Santiago to play drums and banjo, respectively. He had not done so by the morning of the session, so Robinson sent a message to Rogers and brought along his friend Lawrence Marrero to play banjo. Most of these men had regular day jobs, because music was not a paying profession in New Orleans at that time, but they were only too glad to finish early to

George Lewis

join in the music-making. Neither of the recording studios in the city would have anything to do with negro musicians, but an assistant in Grunewald's music store produced a recording machine and a box of acetates and allowed them to use a piano store on the third floor. They moved the pianos around to make a space for the band, and placed boxes and coats to break up reflected sound.

Hal McIntyre was so appalled by the condition of Lewis's clarinet that he brought along another instrument for him to play. Russell thought that George used it because he did not want to offend McIntyre, but he had trouble playing it in tune and did not sound as good as he had on his own instrument. Nevertheless, the music was impressive in its earthy vitality, the like of which the enthusiasts had never before experienced. Owing to the difficulty of achieving a balance with the single microphone, the band's first attempts were unsuccessful, but after the first version of *Yes, Lord, I'm crippled* had run off the end of the disc nine titles were recorded straight off. As the recording went on a crowd gathered in the street outside to listen, and people working in the store came up to the third floor to hear the band.

Bunk's trumpet playing is astonishing in its aptness and authority. While not all the notes are hit correctly, his lead is splendid in its supple invention of variations, his attack is direct and full of urgency and his tone is as fine and true as could possibly be expected from a man playing in public for the first time in years; there is no sense of caution, of holding anything back. All his work is close to the melody, but full of variety. The band backs him with great spirit. Lewis, though a little uncomfortable on the borrowed clarinet, binds the ensemble with his liquid fire and provides much of the emotion, while Robinson plays in the only way he knew, with thrusting, unselfish energy. The rhythm is heavy and hypnotic, driven by Rogers's parade-style drumming. The constricted recording crowds the instruments together, but it also welds them into a single dynamic entity. Decou can hardly be heard and the trombone is muffled, but Lewis is clear enough and Bunk, the special object of attention, comes over with splendid impact.

Perhaps the best of the titles from this first session is *Moose March*, which is full of colour and atmosphere. Bunk uses all his expertise to propel the music forward and the rest of the band responds with great exuberance. This is jazz reduced to its fundamentals, played by men whose styles were comparatively unaffected by the preceding 20 years, and recorded on equipment that emphasised raw vitality at the expense of subtlety. The music, however, is by no means primitive. Some of its excitement derives from the fact that it is a collective activity shaped during its conception and not predetermined. In this it may be labelled a folk music, as it is a product of a common social heritage in which the listener has as active a part as the performer. Bunk, Lewis and the other members of the band were playing against, as much as with, each other. The resulting heterophony leaves no doubt that this spontaneous, clashing sound must have been a part of New Orleans music since the time of Buddy Bolden.

The results of the Jazz Man session, along with an episode recorded on the same day of Bunk reminiscing, have been reissued on LP on the Good Time Jazz label. We are actually fortunate to be able to hear these recordings, for when Stuart sent the acetates to Los Angeles for processing, an engineer thought they sounded so bad that he nearly threw them away. From the standpoint of the quality of studio recordings of the time they are certainly crude, but it is still possible to get a lot of joy out of them, and in the circumstances it is remarkable that they sound as good as they do. Russell, enraptured by the music, thought that with a bit of care he could obtain a better recorded sound, and his chance to prove it came a little later.

In October 1942 Gene Williams was once again in New Orleans and he recorded Bunk and his band in the San Jacinto Hall. The resulting sound quality is a little smoother than that of the recordings from the earlier session, and so is the music. There is no evidence that Bunk had worked with the other musicians in the meantime. He had returned to New Iberia, while Lewis was supporting his young family by working as a stevedore at the docks, taking occasional music jobs at Luthjens dance hall with Billie and De De Pierce. Jim Robinson was not available, so the brass-band expert Albert Warner was called in to play trombone. Decou and Marrero from the previous session were involved, as were Chester Zardis on bass and Edgar Mosley on drums. Bunk's playing emphasises melodic variation and is noticeably less raw than before. It is not fair to call Warner's playing crude, for, although basic, it is an expert embodiment of brass-band principles. Although he lacks the energy of Robinson, his spare playing leaves Bunk plenty of space to develop his lead and is particularly effective in the ragtime numbers. Lewis plays in his usual lyrical way, fitting his long-drawn-out notes, runs and arabesques around the trumpet. The recording balance shows more of the finesse of the rhythm section than that of the Jazz Man session, with Decou's solid piano is well in evidence.

The tunes in this session for Jazz Information reflect Bunk's outlook better than those of the earlier date, when he was restricted to numbers that his sidemen could play at short notice. There are two rags, an old Hawaiian song, an Irving Berlin ballad, the Louis Armstrong trumpet speciality *Shine* and a pretty

San Jacinto Hall,
New Orleans

sentimental number, *Blue Bells, Goodbye*. Traditional blues and a spiritual are also represented. Bunk gives all this material his own stamp, using the range of material to parade his flexibility of variation and melodic invention. The results are charming, and rather old-fashioned; they are less fiercely vital than the Jazz Man recording, but they have a great deal more light and shade. Distribution was entrusted to Milt Gabler of Commodore Records, and an early LP appeared on that label (although the original 78s were labelled Jazz Information); they are presently available on Commodore, and also on Cadillac with the benefit of Williams's original notes.

After this second session Bunk once again retired to New Iberia; he said that New Orleans was a dirty city and that he never wanted

53

to live there again. It seems a pity that he did not prolong his involvement in the musical life of the place, which, although not flourishing, still had some activity. He would not, however, have approved of the sort of work that was most generally available – playing an endless succession of tunes at taxi dances, where the punters paid by the dance and the management obliged the musicians to keep the numbers short. The existing incumbents of the more congenial, though equally scruffy, social dance halls such as Luthjens, Happy Landings and the Moulin Rouge over in Algiers jealously maintained their tenure. At that time Bourbon Street, which owed its later popularity with the jostling tourists to the nationwide rejuvenation of the New Orleans scene of which Bunk was a part, was just another haven for strippers. Nevertheless, with the appearance of the recording and the prolific writings of Bill Russell, Eugene Williams and others, Bunk was now something of a celebrity among the jazz intelligentsia, and it was impossible that he would be allowed to disappear from public view again.

CHAPTER 6

CALIFORNIA, HERE I COME!

The collecting of early jazz records became something of a cult at the end of the 1930s, and such groups as Bob Crosby's orchestra and its small band-within-a-band, the Bobcats, which used material from the 1920s and original compositions in a similar style and which employed in its ranks some distinguished white New Orleans musicians, became extremely successful. As a consequence of this cult there emerged in San Francisco some groups that attempted to play in the old manner. One of the earliest to lead such a group along these lines was the trumpeter Lu Watters, whose Yerba Buena Jazz Band attempted to emulate the style of King Oliver in particular. The effect was not improved by an addiction to the brass bass played in an over-emphatic way, which became the trade-mark of this and other San Fransico bands. One of these was the group led later by Watter's trombonist, Turk Murphy. Murphy was a strong adherent of the style of Kid Ory, who had recently begun playing again in Los Angeles. Watter's clarinettist Ellis Horne idolised Johnny Dodds. The Yerba Buena Band made some recording for Dave Stuart's Jazz Man label.

In early 1943 Rudi Blesh, who was on the fringe of the movement associated with the book *Jazzmen*, arranged to give a series of lectures on New Orleans jazz at the Museum of Art in San Francisco. He felt that these should be accompanied by live music, and that Bunk Johnson was the ideal man to give the exercise real meaning. He raised money by subscription, and, with Bill Russell's help, got Bunk to the West Coast. Bunk arrived late and without any luggage, explaining that it had been stolen along with his hotel reservation. Mutt Carey, who, by a strange coincidence, was a porter on the train Bunk did arrive on, helped him to find lodgings. Fortunately he still had his trumpet, and was just in time for the concert, where he made a great impression both by his playing and

Turk Murphy

by his charming and confident manner. Although his late arrival suggests some sort of deviation along the way, his drinking does not seem to have caused any problems at that time.

Blesh had also recruited Bertha Gonsoulin, a lady who had once played with King Oliver in Chicago, but was by then heavily involved in church music, to accompany Bunk on the piano. Also with Gonsoulin, he made some recordings soon after his arrival in San Francisco. There were four long takes of *Pallet on the Floor* with Bunk purporting to play after the manner of Buddy Bolden, ragging the melody with purposeful flourishes, and three titles in his own style, which are a little lack-lustre. At the same time he recorded another of his interviews, where he talked about Bolden and whistled in his style: he also remembered Pete Lala's and Dago Tony's saloons and, in a rather deliberate manner on the piano, played the tune he claimed to have helped Tony Jackson compose. All these recordings were later issued on Bill Russell's American Music label and subsequently on Dan in Japan.

56

At this time a startling sound reached the ears of the New Orleans enthusiasts, who were by now accustomed to the rather retrospective effect of Bunk Johnson's trumpet. Bill Russell went to New Orleans to record Bunk and found that he had just left for San Francisco. Undeterred, he used what had become known as Bunk's band, but with Kid Howard in place of the missing leader. What transpired was an altogether less stately sort of music, with Howard attacking notes with great force and, as one critic put it, using 'a vibrato as wide as a barn door'. The recordings, credited to George Lewis and his New Orleans Stompers, caused a great sensation at the time and have since become as distinguished in the annals of New Orleans jazz as those by Bunk himself. They showed that Bunk was not the only worthy trumpet player in the city, and also that time had not stood still during the years since he was in his prime.

The music is by no means as organised as was Bunk's ideal, but it has an instinctive co-operative cohesion and, with Howard playing as he rarely did later, is very exhilarating indeed. It shows, too, that Lewis could play with more flair and expression in a band where he could exercise his own confident authority, and where he had more space than Bunk's tight conceptions would allow him. The recordings were offered by Russell to Alfred Lion and Francis Wolfe of Blue Note, who were delighted to take them up because there was a ban on commercial recording at the time; they issued them on the Climax label so that their source would not be obvious to the musicians' union. On the previous day Russell also recorded some rehearsal tracks without Howard and with Sidney Brown (also known as Jim Little) on brass bass in place of Chester Zardis. One of these titles, *Two Jim Blues*, featuring Little and Robinson, was sent to San Francisco where Bunk was recorded playing over it; retitled *Pacific Street Blues*, it was not a great success.

Bill Russell followed Bunk to the West Coast, where he, Blesh and Bill Colburn set about organising another concert to feature the trumpeter. Kid Ory and others had formed a band in Los Angeles in response to the revival of interest in New Orleans jazz. Only a sporadic group at that time, it later became as famous as Bunk's as a result of broadcasting regularly on Orson Welles's radio show. Ory rounded up his old bassist friend Ed Garland, the pianist Buster Wilson and the drummer Alton Redd. His former clarinettist Wade Whaley was unearthed in San Francisco, and Mutt Carey was also roped in. Bunk was played an old record featuring Ory to remind him of the trombonist's style. There was a lot of trouble in organising the concert, because the local white union insisted that a Caucasian group should also be used, but that no racial intermixing be allowed on the stage. Musically, however, the concert seems to have been a great success; a high point came when, on *Maryland, my Maryland*, Bunk and Mutt traded phrases with one another from where each was standing on the stage and the balcony. The union's ruling seems to have been ignored for the finale, as the Yerba Buena men joined in with Bunk and Ory's band on the stage.

While in San Francisco Bunk was heard by Virgil Thomson, composer and music critic of the *New York Herald-Tribune*. Thomson was very impressed by Bunk's playing, and the publicity he gave him kept the nationwide interest in the trumpeter on the boil. The San Francisco Hot Jazz Society promoted him with the Yerba Buena sidemen at the hall of the Longshoremen's Union on Sunday evenings. Lu Watters was not among them, however, having been conscripted into the navy, and it is not clear whether his trumpet partner, Bob Scobey, was involved in these sessions or whether Bunk led them on his own. Mutual admiration between Bunk and the members of the band was not complete; they were puzzled by his determination to play such ephemerally popular tunes as *Mairzy Doats*, and by his tendency to teach them how to play New Orleans music when they considered themselves experts on the subject. Bunk seems to have played as he wanted to, regardless of what the band was doing, but eventually his example told and the sidemen fell into place behind him. Sometimes Bunk's drinking became a problem and he failed to turn up, but generally he made a good impression. He was in demand for social occasions and revelled in his popularity, impressing his hosts and their guests with his charm, his wit and his articulate eloquence. And he was not at all averse to flirting elegantly with the ladies.

In early 1944 Bunk, without any great show of willingness on his part, was persuaded by David Rosenbaum of the San Francisco Hot Jazz Society to make some recording with the Yerba Buena musicians. These were made over several sessions, and apparently Bunk sometimes declined to turn up or forgot to bring his trumpet. By no means all the results were issued, and those that were took a long time to come out. The group is not particularly homogeneous, with its lumbering rhythm section and incomplete ensemble unanimity, but the recording is good enough to let the listener appreciate the excellence of Bunk's tone and the subtleties of his timing. *Careless Love* shows him at his most impressive, playing lucid and logical variations on the old theme. It also shows that his expressiveness was entirely musical, unlike that of later trumpet players who almost literally shouted, cried and laughed through their horns. Bunk let the music speak through his trumpet in the good old-fashioned way, an embodiment equally of his position in the evolution of jazz and of his detached and individual attitude to life.

In one of the Yerba Buena sessions the gospel singer Sister

Lottie Peavey was brought in to perform some traditional hymns. She would put up with no nonsense from Bunk, and he responded with some fine work to back her magnificent singing. When it came to recording *Down by the Riverside*, Lottie did not think that the words were religious enough for her to sing, so Bunk took over the vocal instead, incorporating variations of inflection and timing as he was wont to do on the trumpet. Although the recording sessions had some fruitful results, (best heard on Good Time Jazz), they stretched the relationship between Bunk and the band to breaking point, and, in any case, difficulties were still being raised over his playing with white musicians. He worked on the waterfront and as a storeman, writing back to Weeks Hall for a reference. He played some gigs with Baker Millian, his saxophonist friend from western Louisiana, who had settled on the West Coast. By the middle of 1944 Bunk's patience with San Francisco wore out, and he set off back to New Iberia.

The Yerba Buena Jazz Band: Turk Murphy (trombone), Lu Walters (trumpet), Bob Scobey (trumpet), Bob Helm (clarinet) and Dick Lammi (tuba)

On his way home Bunk stopped off in Los Angeles to do some recording for the World Transcription Service, which the Decca recording company used to provide material for radio stations. The band, which was recruited by Bill Colburn, was made up of experienced professional musicians under the title of Bunk's' V-disc Veterans. Wade Whaley was, of course, already known to Bunk. On trombone there was Floyd O'Brien, late of the Bob

Crosby band. The pianist Fred Washington had recorded with Kid Ory in 1922 and the guitarist Frank Pasley, from New Orleans, had recorded with Preston Jackson in Chicago in the 1920s. The other two were relative modernists, Red Callender on bass and Lester Young's brother Lee on drums; to the latter's great astonishment, Bunk remembered taking him to school in New Orleans. They all thought that they would be condescending to a spent musician, but Bunk soon showed them otherwise.

The music shows Bunk in better-organised surroundings than before, in a band where the musicians were disciplined enough to keep in their proper places, and presents well his quite delicate, thoughtful way of making music. By this time he had his technique well under control, and was able to play his elaborate variations on the lead smoothly and precisely. He is the dominant figure, while the others play efficiently but without much fire. Whaley has an appealing style, but a rather diffident approach and approximate execution, while O'Brien does little more than fill in. Nevertheless, as a group to support the trumpeter it was more than adequate, and evidently more to his liking than bands made up of the less professional, but more enthusiastic, musicians in New Orleans. The tunes reflect his demand for variety: there is the New Orleans society number *Mama's Gone, Goodbye*, the long-forgotten rag *Spicy Advice* and the old vaudeville song *Akansas Blues*, along with several items which he had recorded before. Particularly interesting is the dixieland standard *I ain't gonna give nobody none of my jelly roll*, popular at that time because Tommy Ladnier had also recorded it five years earlier; comparison between the two versions shows that the trumpeters' playing had something basic in common.

The recordings from the World Transcription session first became available to the English enthusiast on Purist, the label of the Bunk Johnson Appreciation Society, and have since appeared on an LP on the NoLa label. Bunk also took part in a broadcast with the Kid Ory band while in Los Angeles. Although not officially issued, four titles from the occasion have circulated; the first three are by the regular band, with Mutt Carey alone on trumpet, but Bunk can be heard adding his appealing blues playing in lead and solo to *Basin Street Blues*. However, he was kicking the dust of the West Coast out of his well-travelled shoes. He had an appointment in New Orleans with Bill Russell, and between them the two men were to make some of the best-loved and most influential recordings of the New Orleans renaissance.

CHAPTER 7

AMERICAN MUSIC

Before he set out again for New Orleans, Bill Russell had equipped himself with a second-hand Federal disc recorder and a quantity of glass-based acetate discs. At first the recorder would not work, but fortunately Russell had a brother who was an engineer, who made it servicable. In the meantime George Lewis had been playing with Herb Morand in a band which the visiting jazz writer Kenneth Hulsizer thought was the best group he heard playing New Orleans music in the city; since his other experiences were of hearing Kid Rena, long past his best, and the well drilled big band of Sidney Desvigne, this is hardly surprising. With George and Herb were Eddie Morris, a trombonist who had been in Punch Miller's successful band before the latter left the city, and a bass player called 'Slow Drag', who apparently had no distinguished past but was able to provide the sort of strong rhythm that Lewis liked.

When Russell arrived Lewis was suffering from the effects of two accidents in the docks, in one of which a truck hit him in the chest. But he was able to play with the help of medication, and Russell set up the recorder in his bedroom, where the clarinettist, along with his friend Lawrence Marrero on banjo and Slow Drag on bass, put on acetate one of the best-loved of all New Orleans recordings. To Lewis it was just a blues, but the record had to have a name, and after considering various titles Eugene Williams dubbed it *Burgundy Street Blues* (pronounced in New Orleans with the second syllable emphasised), after the street where both the rhythm men lived. Later, while touring, Lewis was never allowed to appear without playing this famous number, in his hands one of the most moving of all instrumental blues. The group also recorded two other tunes and a brief passage with Lewis on the flute.

When Lewis told him Slow Drag's surname, Russell thought it sounded like 'Novello'. He later found out that the bassist's name was Alcide Pavageau and that his nickname was earned by his

expertise in the dance of the same name. His method of playing was unorthodox and, some would say, primitive. He obtained the strong, percussive sound that is so impressive on recordings by using a very low bridge and pulling the strings so that they sprang back and hit the soundboard. Along with Marrero, he made up a very strong, emphatic rhythm team. Russell brought down Baby Dodds, who had impressed him greatly in Chicago, to play drums; Dodds used the kit of a local drummer, Abby Williams.

When Bunk was back in New Iberia, Russell went over to see him at his home, 638 Franklin Street. He was barefoot in ragged overalls, cleaning up the grass and weeds around his house with an improvised sickle. He showed Russell his pride and joy, his old Ford car, and told him that he regularly ground the valves, helped by his tame Cuban monkey. He also showed Russell around The Shadows. Russell was astonished by some fast technical exercises on the trumpet, which led Bunk to declare his admiration for Louis Armstrong's playing. Russell asked whether Bunk agreed that Louis, at that time, would not be able to take his place in a New Orleans group and Bunk said that, of course, Armstrong's approach was different. He went on to say: 'Anybody that thinks

Lawrence Marrero, George Lewis and Slow Drag Pavageau outside Lewis's house in Burgundy Street, New Orleans

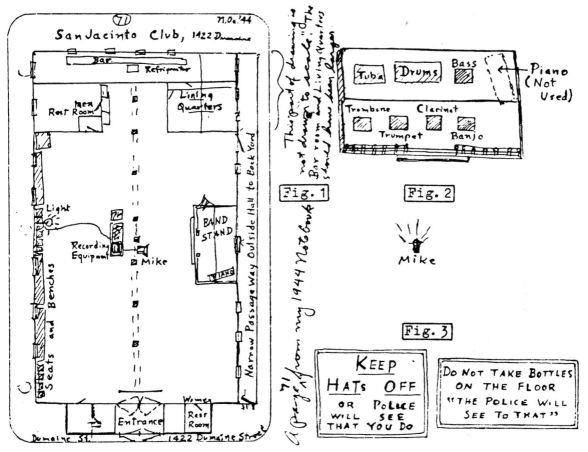

The sketch contains the following handwritten labels:

71   n.d. '44

San Jacinto Club, 1422 Dumaine

Bar

Refrigerator

Men Rest Room

Living Quarters

Light

Recording Equipment

Mike

BAND STAND

PIANO

Seats and Benches

Narrow Passage Way Outside Hall to Back Yard

Women Rest Room

Entrance

Dumaine St.   1422 Dumaine Street

This part of drawing not drawn to scale; "d" The Bar room and Living Quarters stood have been larger

Fig. 1

(A page 71 from my 1944 Note Book

Fig. 2

Tuba   Drums   Bass   ← Piano (Not Used)

Trombone   Clarinet

Trumpet   Banjo

Mike

Fig. 3

KEEP HATS OFF
OR   POLICE
WILL   SEE
THAT YOU DO

DO NOT TAKE BOTTLES
ON THE FLOOR
"THE POLICE WILL
SEE TO THAT"

Bill Russell's sketch of San Jacinto Hall for the American Music recordings, 1944

they can outplay Louis, send them around to me; if I can't outplay 'em, I can talk 'em to death. Yes, if I can't outplay him, I can out-talk him.'

Bunk moved to New Orleans and stayed at Abby Williams's home, and a week-long recording session was undertaken at the San Jacinto Hall; its warm resonance proved ideal for sound purposes, and it has since been used for many fine sessions. The recording was to take place in the early evening, to fit in with the musicians who had day jobs and to allow them to fulfil dance engagements afterwards. Russell had by then equipped himself with a second recorder as back-up, and his younger brother to operate it. Only one microphone was used with each machine, and these were set up on two chairs about 15 feet in front of the bandstand. Bunk was placed in the middle, to get the best use of the microphone. The first evening, 30th July 1944, was intended to be a rehearsal; for some reason Pavageau was not available, and Sidney Brown took his place, playing tuba. Bunk wanted to play popular tunes of the 1920s and started off with one called *Yes, yes in your eyes,* which he performed very strongly; evidently his lip had benefited from his time in California. The only title from this session that has been issued is *Lowdown Blues*, which shows that the band was playing well together, that the leader was in fine authoritative form and that Baby Dodds was giving the group a great lift.

The next day's work was complicated by the fact that Bunk, who took the business of recording less seriously than the others and showed virtually no interest in listening to the playbacks, was into his routine of touring the New Orleans saloons, drinking and talking to old friends. The rest of the band had to make *San Jacinto Stomp* before he deigned to turn up, but this proved to be a bonus because it pointed the way to a format that was used successfully later with just Lewis and Robinson in the front line.

When Bunk did arrive, the results were fine. Brown's tuba playing was satisfactory, though not ideal for that kind of group; he also played string bass, if rather weakly, on some numbers. Dodds, with his superb bass drumming, was well able to make up for Brown, while the rock-like Marrero provided a basic beat and Robinson contributed his unique propulsion. Several titles were made with a singer, Myrtle Jones – possibly on the basis of the success of Bunk's partnership with Sister Lottie Peavey. With her sharp, aggressive voice, she was by no means Peavey's equal, but she was more catholic in her attitude, performing quite well enough in both gospel and blues modes and reflecting the warm empathy of the band.

The evening finished with some excellent instrumental sides: *St Louis Blues*, with Lewis showing fully his expressive capabilities, a dynamic version of *Tiger Rag* with superb drum work from Dodds, and an intense rendition of *New Iberia Blues*, in one passage of which Lewis remarked that Bunk sounded just like Buddy Petit. Everything augured well for the next evening's work, but Bunk's contradictory nature again came into play. In the morning he said that he wanted to buy a hat, and wandered off. By the time the other musicians set out for the hall he was still absent and Russell and Lewis went to look for him. When they found him he was staggering out of a bar, and after they got him to the hall he could not play much. Although they recorded a number of titles, the session was more or less a washout – apart from a long blues which they recorded (at 33⅓ r.p.m.) after Bunk had sobered up. LP records were not being made at that time, and they did not know if it would ever be issued, but Alfred Lion heard it and reckoned it was worth 100 dollars; Russell retorted that it had cost him a good deal more than that!

Bunk evidently had a conscience of a sort, or else was afraid to aggravate his benefactor too much. The next evening he was the first to be ready to record and played beautifully throughout the session. Slow Drag was present, adding to the depth of the rhythm.

Bunk Johnson, 1944

They started off with *The Saints*, already made popular by Louis Armstrong but at that time by no means the hackneyed warhorse it was to become. Bunk's lead is exemplary in its drive and variety, Lewis sings like a nightingale and Robinson plays his customary supporting role perfectly. Two takes were made, both equally successful. The session continued in this impressive manner through to a superb nine-minute blues, in which Bunk parades all his know-how in an entirely logical construction that never wears out its welcome. During the evening Baby Dodds likened the trumpeter's playing to that of Manuel Perez and the following day

65

Bunk went to visit his old fellow-cornettist, who had long retired from music. A year earlier Perez had suggested to Russell that if Bunk could make a comeback, so could he; now he was confused to find Bunk playing again. Evidently his mental state was well into the decline which left him, for the rest of his life, sitting in a chair and staring into space.

That evening our hero fulfilled his wish to put *Yes, yes in your eyes* on record, and the tune fitted the band, spurred on by Dodd's inventive drumming, just as well as the more traditional material. All went well, as well as the previous night, with Bunk providing perhaps a little more edge to his trumpet work to add to the excitement. This edge, however, may have come from the fact that Bunk was losing patience with his regular obligation to devote his evenings to recording; he did not consider the sessions all that important except as a means to get him public work in the North. By the end of the fourth day he sounds as if he is losing either energy or interest. On the Friday morning, Russell found that Bunk had left the Williams's house, saying that he was going to the barber's. Knowing the reputation of barbers in New Orleans, Russell feared that this meant another boozing session. In the afternoon he and Lewis set off for South Rampart Street, which Bunk had mentioned, to search the barbershops and saloons. They saw Bunk standing in front of the Astoria Hotel, swinging a gold watch (which, it transpired, he had just bought for 30 dollars) on its chain. Not wanting to look as if they were hunting him, they pretended to have met him by chance, but he was not fooled. They tried to get him into a taxi so that he could eat at George's house before the session, but he said he would meet them at the hall; having been caught out like that before, they persisted and Bunk did go with them, but he had his meal and fell asleep in a rocking chair.

Fearful of waking Bunk too soon, Russell let Lewis go ahead to prepare for the recording, taking Bunk's trumpet with him. When woken at the last minute, Bunk was enraged that they should have parted him from his horn and refused to go the hall with Russell, who was very embarrassed by all this hassle with a man whom he respected as an artist and wanted to respect as a responsible person. He left it to Lewis and the others to go and search for Bunk. They found him once more in a bar, but he came with them quite willingly; they felt, however, that he would probably have stayed in the bar all evening had he not been fetched. Not surprisingly, only two titles from that session were considered by Russell to be worth issuing, although others have appeared since. During the recording a young sailor whom Bunk had been teaching in New Iberia turned up at the hall. Afterwards Bunk would not eat with the band but went on the town with the sailor; he also

Bunk Johnson's Band, from the left: Jim Robinson, Bunk, Baby Dodds, George Lewis

intended to visit him next day. He clearly meant to go on a bender.

The other members of the band were getting fed up with being messed about by their nominal leader, so Russell decided to find another trumpet player for the Saturday evening. At this time Russell seems to have had one main idea in mind, to record as much of Bunk's playing as he possibly could, and he seems to have had no interest in using other musicians in the band. Subsequent events have shown that he was in the vicinity of a wealth of talent, but the musicians he did use were probably just about as good as he could have found and answered his requirements of ability and temperament well. In the event Kid Shots Madison, Louis Armstrong's old friend from the Waifs Home, was selected as Bunk's replacement because he was well known to the rest of the band. We must be glad that he was, because Shots was a good trumpeter who offered a definite stylistic contrast and yet fitted in with the others at least as well as Bunk did.

Since his work with Papa Celestin in the 1920's, Madison had become a brass-band specialist. He had a good deal of vibrato and a lazy way of phrasing, in which he could sway about the beat, playing long, slow notes interspersed with runs somewhat in the manner of Chris Kelly's followers, but without the fierce attack of Kid Howard. Like Bunk, he definitely preferred to stay in mid-

67

Bunk with Baby Dobbs and Jim Robinson, Burgundy Street, New Orleans

range, and made a lovely warm sound. It has to be said that his version of the old hymn *Over in the Gloryland* has a good deal more fervour, for all its gentleness, than Bunk's. His character seems to have been the opposite of Bunk's, for he was diffident and anxious to please, and modest of his own capabilities. He was very effective, though, particularly on the slow drag *Bucket's got a hole in it* and the pretty popular tune *When you and I were young, Maggie,* which the band had wanted to record all week. He played the blues beautifully too. The whole evening's work was a great success, and probably much less wearing on everybody's nerves than the previous ones.

Shots had to leave early to go on a job, so Russell took the opportunity to record some more sides with just Lewis and Robinson in the front line. He was rewarded with a beautiful blues named after San Jacinto Hall, and then somebody suggested the frivolous song *Ice Cream.* Russell did not know that this was a New Orleans trombone speciality, and was astonished when Robinson came out of his predictable mode to express himself strongly and eloquently. Lewis easily carried the responsibilities of leadership, being accustomed to do so in his band when Herb Morand failed to turn up, and the spare texture allowed Baby Dodds to be heard in all his glory.

All in all, Bill Russell was very satisfied with his week's work, and he was right to be. The distinguished jazz aficionado John Hammond, who had worked for Columbia Records but was then in the army, turned up at the hall on one of the evenings, and said he thought that the results would be the best recordings ever made in New Orleans. That may be putting it a little strongly, but after 40 years it is possible to say that they are among the very best and owing to the time at which they were made, undoubtedly the most influential. Russell put the best of them out on 78s and latterly, on

Baby Dodds, 1944

LP on his American Music label. More recently they have been taken over by Storyville and Dan, which have reissued all the well-known material and have also made available a good deal of the previously rejected music.

After the sessions were over Bunk went on a week-long spree in New Orleans on the proceeds, though he told Bill Russell during the week that he had sent some of the money home. When he got back to New Iberia he sent a cordial letter to Lewis, saying that his wife was giving him hell for not coming straight home. He was looking forward to playing with George again soon, and sent regards to his family. Evidently, when in a rational mood Bunk was very satisfied with their musical relationship, but his independent spirit may well have been irked by the fact that the clarinettist had been Russell's chief aide in keeping him in line.

Lewis, in his turn, clearly admired Bunk's trumpet playing, finding in it a quality missing from the work of younger men. He may of course have been seeking to please Russell, for that was his nature; he was, after all, perfectly content to play with such musicians as Kid Howard and De De Pierce for the rest of his life, and he made some marvellous music with them. Nevertheless, there was a great deal to admire in Bunk's revived musicianship; his attitude towards his profession was far more thorough and thoughtful than that of the general run of New Orleans musicians of that time, who tended to rely on an instinctive, ad hoc, approach. It is nice to think, however, that Bunk also appreciated Lewis's more homespun, but nonetheless valid, virtues. In his own way he does seem to have been grateful to Bill Russell for being the chief instigator of his rescue from oblivion and the immortalisation of his playing, at least in the sense that it had elevated him to the status of something of a celebrity among the jazz intelligentsia.

CHAPTER 8

BUNK AND BECHET IN BOSTON

In 1940 Sidney Bechet had been involved in an abortive attempt to bring Bunk Johnson up to New York to take part in a recording session for Victor. This may have been a gesture to please his brother Leonard, who was anxious to get some mileage out of the teeth he had made for Bunk. In any case, Bunk was clearly not ready for such an outing at that time. The plan had to be kept secret, lest Victor should find out that a non-union musician was to take part in one of their sessions, and Sidney had a ready-made excuse to scrap the venture when Bunk spilled the beans to Louis Armstrong, who told the press. Bechet also used the situation to foster his dislike of Eugene Williams who, he claimed, had turned Bunk off the idea because he wanted him to record in New Orleans first. Bunk, in his turn, told Sidney that he agreed to record for Williams and Bill Russell only because they got him drunk, but the fact that the Jazz Man session took place two years later makes a nonsense of this. Clearly, there was not much integrity on either side of the deal. In the event Rex Stewart played cornet in the Victor session and made a very good job of it.

In January 1945 a concert was arranged in the New Orleans Municipal Auditorium. This was to celebrate the restoration of Basin Street's original name (which, because of its unsavoury past, had been changed to North Saratoga Street). The concert was sponsored by *Esquire* magazine, and was broadcast as part of a nationwide jazz programme featuring the winners of the magazine's jazz poll of the previous year. The New Orleans performers were to be Louis Armstrong, Sidney Bechet, Paul Barbarin on drums, Ricard Alexis – no longer able to play trumpet – on bass, the trombonist J. C. Higginbotham (born in Georgia), and the New York pianist James P. Johnson. (Also involved in the concert was a white band led by the trumpeter Leon Prima.) Russell and Williams had inveigled their way onto the poll panel in

Bunk with Louis Armstrong

order to ensure that Bunk got some votes, and the climax was to be a performance of *Basin Street Blues* with Bunk joining the Armstrong group. Unfortunately, earlier proceedings took longer than expected, and the broadcast was cut short in the middle of this climax. On the resulting air-shot Bunk plays a melodious obbligato behind Armstrong's vocal, and the two trumpeters can be heard faintly exchanging phrases behind the closing announcements; apparently they continued to play together for some time after the broadcast ended.

Sidney Bechet was very keen to assemble an old-style New Orleans group. He had been involved in Hugues Panassié's recording sessions with Tommy Ladnier and had tried to organise a band around the two of them, but had been frustrated by the trumpeter's death in 1939. He discussed the idea of teaming up Bunk with John Reid and Rudi Blesh, who were encouraging. Sidney mentioned this to Leonard when he was in New Orleans, but the latter was doubtful, thinking that recording for Bill Russell had given Bunk over-ambitious ideas which would make him difficult to control. Nevertheless, it was arranged that Bunk should join Bechet for an engagement at the Savoy Café in Boston.

72

Before Bunk went north, a rather bizarre event occurred in New Orleans that led to a further recording session by the 'American Music' band. Probably at the instigation of John Hammond, the Office of War Information commissioned a film involving the visit of eight members of the French Resistance, including the philosopher Jean-Paul Sartre, to New Orleans, the American offshoot of their cultural heritage. It seems to have been a rather slapdash affair. A jazz enthusiast, Gus Statiras, who had worked in a record shop and knew Hammond, was passing through New Orleans at the time on the way to a posting in Texas. He was asked by Orin Blackstone, on behalf of the newly formed New Orleans Jazz Society, to record Bunk and the band as background music. Statiras had never actually handled a recorder before, although he had watched Hammond do it, but he agreed to do the one title if he was allowed to keep the acetate after the film people had finished with it. He made contact with George Lewis, and got to know his family. Bunk arrived from New Iberia and the band had a rehearsal – but without a drummer because Baby Dodds was back in Chicago. Eventually a replacement was found in Abby Williams, who was not a very good drummer but was a shrewd businessman who had secured Lewis many jobs in the past.

Statiras made the recordings in the studio of a radio station; it

The French Quarter, 1940s

seems that all he had to do was to place the single microphone and direct the proceedings. Although the organisation wanted only *Tiger Rag*, the band actually made four titles. Having completed the recording, everyone went round to the St Charles Hotel, where the Frenchmen and a number of jazz enthusiasts were gathered, and the band was filmed playing *Tiger Rag* again. When the film was edited, the solos were identified with the wrong instruments and the whole thing was a mess. Russell and Williams saw the film shortly afterwards, but thereafter it seems to have disappeared without trace. Statiras kept the acetates, but he never played them and they were later sold to Bill Grauer, who put them out on Metronome and then on his own Riverside label. The drummer was identified as Kid Collins, probably because no one had documented his name and one had to be made up. Statiras said that the drumming made him cringe, and for that reason, as well as a distorted recording, the results do not compare at all favourably with the American Music recordings. On the night before the session the musicians had all stayed at Lewis's house. Statiras shared a bed with Bunk. It was so cold that they kept all their clothes on – shoes, overcoats, hats and all.

Bunk went to New York shortly after the film session. One of the first things he did on arrival was to take part in a recording date with Bechet for Blue Note. Sandy Williams was on trombone and impressed Bunk with his command of the instrument. Probably competing with Bechet, the trumpeter was hitting higher notes than usual, but, in deference to the retrospective philosophy of the session, Bechet performed on clarinet throughout. Bunk's playing was strong enough to match Bechet's, although his phrasing was noticeably squarer than that of the others. The band recorded two of Bechet's slow blues compositions, similar in style and atmosphere to *Really the Blues* (which Sidney had recorded with Ladnier for Panassié), and some up-tempo numbers in which Bunk's technique is sure and accurate. It is all rewarding music, if rather different to what Bill Russell had been recording. Bunk obviously enjoyed being put on his mettle by a group of sophisticated musicians, and he was not found wanting.

On the day of the Blue Note session Bunk was interviewed by Eddie Condon, who had a show on CBS Radio. On the following day he played with Bechet, Pops Foster, the pianist Hank Duncan and the drummer Freddie Moore in one of Jack Crystal's Sunday Jam Sessions at Jimmy Ryan's Club on 52nd Street. Sandy Williams played trombone in their first set and George Lugg, a Condon associate, in the second. Less the trombone, this was the band that Bechet hoped to take to Boston. By all accounts Bunk played very well, particularly in the second set and certainly well enough to impress the well-known trumpeter Louis Metcalf, who was in the audience. At the end Bunk joined Metcalf and another talented trumpet player, Bobby Stark, to play *Bugle Call Rag*, and he held his head high in the distinguished company. He also made a great impression as a showman and was the centre of a throng of admirers, both enthusiasts and musicians.

Sidney Bechet wrote about the Boston episode in his book *Treat it Gentle* shortly before he died in 1959. He claimed that Eugene Williams was against the idea from the start, wanting Bunk for another job in New York, and that he tried various wiles – first, to prevent Bunk from going to Boston, and second, to break up the band once it was there by getting Bunk drunk. It is true that Williams, with Bill Russell, had been working on a scheme to bring Bunk and his New Orleans band to New York for some time before they knew of the arrangement with Bechet, but correspondence between them and Wynne Paris of the Boston Jazz Society shows that their attitude was, at least initially, one of enthusiastic encouragement. In fact it is quite possible that, had the enterprise been a success, they would have promoted the same band for Bunk in New York.

As it transpired, although Russell was at first too tied to his job in Pittsburgh, and also to his need to get the American Music recordings issued in his spare time, to go to Boston, Williams made several weekend trips there from New York. Depressed by the way things were going between the two main musicians, he made every effort to get them back in tune with each other. Bunk was quite capable of getting himself drunk without any assistance, and Bechet was just as much an individualist and could be equally abrasive; both would modify reality to suit their own egotistical needs for celebrity. It must have irked Bechet that, having travelled all over the world playing in sophisticated orchestras and being acclaimed by high society, he now found himself second in popular attraction to a man who had spent his life in the backwoods.

Although Bechet had played the clarinet in the Blue Note session, it was at that time very much his second instrument. He did not feel that he could express himself on it as well as on the soprano saxophone, the idiosyncratic instrument on which he had forged his unique style. Lacking confidence in Bunk's ability to sustain a reliable trumpet part, he took to playing the soprano more and more; such were his power and exuberance on it, he was a very difficult man for a trumpeter to compete with. Even Louis Armstrong had trouble with Bechet: both in a recording session in 1940 and at the New Orleans concert, the two men had blamed each other for lack of cooperation.

Bechet knew how he wanted music to be played, and so did Bunk, but both were competitive, self-seeking men who knew the

meaning of cooperation only when it was on somebody else's part. Bunk took an instant dislike to Bechet's soprano, calling it a 'fish-horn' and a 'hosepipe', and not troubling to work out a way of dealing with it. Seen with hindsight, he was just not the man for the job.

The venture got off to a bad start. Fred Moore could not be released from his job at Ryan's and Hank Duncan could not make the trip to Boston either. Pops Foster, then working as a porter on the New York subway, was glad to go, and obviously the success of the job meant a lot to him. The other two rhythm men were unknowns: Ray Parker, a rather modern pianist, and George Thompson, an average drummer. The band was to reach Boston on the day after the session at Ryan's and a concert was arranged for that evening, but everything went wrong. First Bechet had to find Bunk, who had been out on the town. He then had to find one of the other members of the band and sober him up. The musicians did not all arrive until the following day, so the concert was cancelled and, presumably, the band started at the Savoy Café on the following night. Taking Bechet's side, Pops Foster said that Bunk got drunk and did not turn up, and blamed Gene Williams for this. Pops sent his wife Alma out looking for Bunk, who turned out to have mislaid his trumpet; she must have given Bunk a good ticking off, for Pops said that he straightened himself out for a while.

Williams, in fact, did not get to Boston until the following weekend because he was working for Decca at the time. He reported to Russell that the band was not very good, although Pops was doing valiantly in making up for the rhythmic deficiencies of the others. Bechet was playing too much soprano for Williams's taste. Bunk spent more time rubbing his lips than actually playing and when he did play he was weak; but the audience seemed to like him. At times, however, Bunk roused himself and played well and then the band sounded good, though not like a New Orleans ensemble. There seems to have been some discussion about bringing in a trombone player, but Bechet thought that they could not afford one.

The reports of Williams, John Reid and others indicate that an assessment of the band's capability depended upon Bunk's mood of the moment, which varied even from one set to another. At times he played very well, while at others he played hardly at all. Bechet, never knowing what was going to happen next, took over the lead, which made Bunk lose interest altogether. Complaints about his teeth led to their sending to Leonard for a new set, but it is not clear whether Bunk used them; if so, they did not make any difference. Sidney, his distrust apparently forgotten, kept asking Williams to talk some sense into Bunk, because the strain of it all

Sidney Bechet

77

was making him ill. There was no reconciling them, however, and the compromise staggered on. On hearing about the situation from Wynne Paris, Bill Russell wrote: '3 good nites out of ten . . . not a very good average'. Bill eventually made his way to Boston, but it was too late. Bunk had finally decided to go home, as he had threatened to do earlier if Sidney would not play as he wanted. He could give up music, he said, since his wife had a job, and he could always fish.

The band made several broadcasts while it was at the Savoy, and most were recorded by a local enthusiast who would attend the first set, rush home to record off the air, and then return to the café to tell the band how it had come over. The most satisfactory broadcast, from the point of view of the music, came when John Reid arrived to see the band during its fourth week in residence. He wanted to record the rehearsal, using the machine previously employed in New Iberia, but he found that the Savoy's electricity supply was DC while the machine worked on AC. By the time he had bought a suitable converter the band was packing up, and in a very sour mood. Despite their unwillingness, he persuaded the musicians to stay and make the recording, and he thought that the aggravation actually made them play better. His results, along with some of the air-shot recordings, have been issued on the Fat Cat label, and the evening's broadcast, with the band still playing well, can be heard on Jazz Archives. Reid hired a studio to record the broadcast, so the sound quality is reasonable. With Bechet the dominant personality, Bunk is by no means outstanding, but it is a partnership with the trumpeter playing consistently and sounding quite relaxed. The same LP includes the broadcast made two nights later, where Bunk sounds sour, inaccurate and uninvolved, though he does go through the motions throughout. He was possibly having difficulty in fitting in with Bechet's phrasing, or, more likely, he was deliberately trying to show that the reedman was playing too many notes.

In Boston, it seems as though Bunk was exercising his well-known prerogative to do exactly what he felt like at any time, unaffected by any sense of responsibility or obligation. He was obviously put out to find that the band was advertised as Bechet's, even though he was the main attraction. He continually expressed the opinion that Bechet did not need a band with a trumpeter, but rather one such as that led by the alto saxophonist Pete Brown, which alternated with theirs at the café. Sidney felt that the condition of Bunk's lip was not a physical problem, but a reflection of his state of mind.

Along with his bitterness, Bechet said that he felt a great sadness when he put his old friend on the train south. He sent to New Orleans for Herb Morand as a replacement, but the latter could

Peter Bocage, 1950

not leave because his mother was ill; Punch Miller was also considered. In the event Peter Bocage, who had made a recording (unissued) for John Reid the previous autumn, came up to Boston to join the band, and in the meantime a young Bostonian trumpeter who was playing in New York, Johnny Windhurst, was brought back as substitute. Bocage did not fit into the band much better than Bunk, and he too tried to tell them how they should play. He was not happy away from home, where he had a steady job, and his tenure was ended by mutual agreement after a short stay. Windhurst completed the residency on a permanent basis.

Ever contradictory, on his return to Louisiana Bunk showed that there was nothing permanently wrong with either his lip or his spirit. Bill Russell was there to witness his extraordinary stamina on a dance job in Pointe à la Hache, down towards the mouth of the Mississippi. He played splendidly with George Lewis's band, continuing into the small hours in response to the local dancers' enthusiasm, with only Slow Drag remaining with the energy to accompany him on the bass drum. The photographer Skippy Adelman was there and, having heard all about Boston, kept expecting Bunk's lip to give out, but it was as strong at the end of the night as it had been at the beginning.

CHAPTER 9

BACK TO NEW ORLEANS

Bill Russell returned to New Orleans after the Boston fiasco with the intention of obtaining a further series of recordings by Bunk Johnson with his 'American Music' band. Bunk, however, remained in New Iberia, helping his wife pack up the belongings of the people she worked for, who were moving to Cuba. In the meantime Russell fulfilled his ambition to record 'Wooden' Joe Nicholas, whose playing he had admired in 1943. The band was another pick-up affair, with Jim Robinson and Lawrence Marrero from Bunk's band. Josiah 'Cié' Frazier was called in to play drums because Baby Dodds had hurt his arm, and Austin Young was on bass. Frazier was a pupil of one of the most famous early drummers, Louis Cottrell Sr, and the clarinettist was Albert Burbank, a Creole who had learnt much from the Tio family and who was known locally as the 'Clarinet Wizard'. Held at Artesian Hall, this was one of the most remarkable New Orleans sessions of all, presenting music rather different from, but the equal of, that recorded by Bunk's band under similar circumstances.

Where Bunk was an intelligent, resourceful trumpeter, Wooden Joe was an instinctive, whole-hearted one. His accomplishment was of a more approximate kind than Bunk's and he was by no means as sophisticated, but he had great power which, when he was on form, carried all before it; and he was certainly on form on that day in May 1945. Both Robinson and Frazier were late arriving, and the rest of the band started out with an inspired version of *Shake it and break it*, with the two front-liners filling all the melodic space and with Young's playing so dynamic that the lack of a drummer is not felt.

The rest of the session fulfilled the promise of its beginning. There was a superbly affectionate rendering of *Careless Love* and other highlights in *Eh la bas*, where Burbank's Creole vocal complements his rippling clarinet work; his solo on *Tiger Rag*

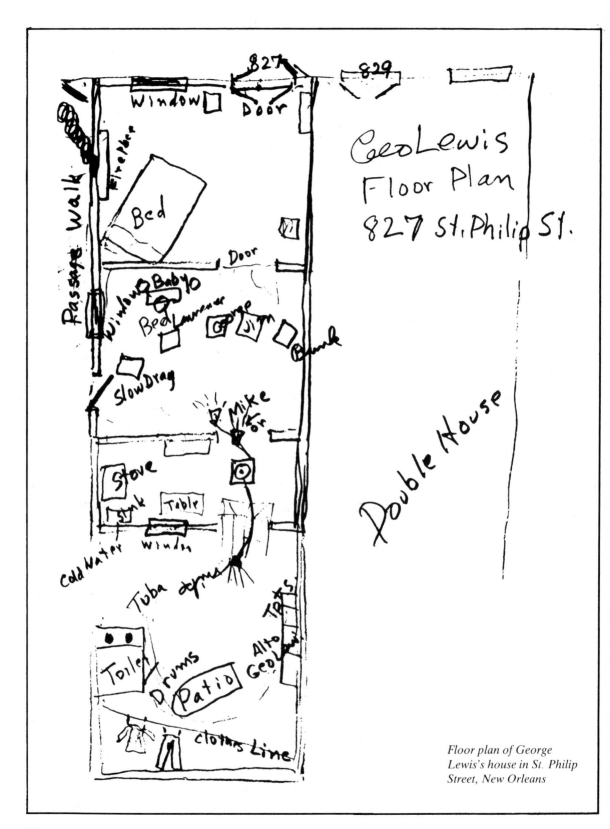

Floor plan of George Lewis's house in St. Philip Street, New Orleans

develops over successive choruses to an almost unbearable climax. Wooden Joe blows his head off throughout, never amiss in timing or tone and always exuberantly rhetorical; he seems to use the sympathetic resonance of the hall as an extension of his trumpet. He plays close to the melody and over the top of the rhythm, often breaking the tune into short fragments or broad, stabbing notes. Burbank fills all the gaps with his fluent, lyrical playing. He is as emotional and rhythmical as George Lewis but more subtle, and though he does not push himself forward the sheer beauty of his work shines out through the spaces in his partner's lead. The session shows quite comprehensively what Wooden Joe had to offer, and we must be profoundly glad of that. It was a fleeting opportunity to document his prime contribution to New Orleans music, while for Burbank, and for Frazier, it was the start of involvements that illuminated many later recordings.

The session did have one unfortunate result. Although, in the view of many delighted enthusiasts, the warm, resonant sound of the recordings seemed perfect, Russell thought that the echo of the hall detracted from the clarity of his results. He therefore decided to hold the rest of his sessions during that visit in George Lewis's home, forgetting that the musicians were accustomed to playing in the ambience of a larger space. Russell is on record as saying that Bunk's band sounded sour that year, although, in a letter to Eugene Williams, he was enthusiastic about the music they played. In comparison with those made in San Jacinto Hall the previous year, the recordings he took at Lewis's house over three nights in May 1945 have a dry, harsh sound which detracts from the listener's enjoyment, although Dodds's drumming skills can be heard with more clarity. Nevertheless, on the first evening some good music was recorded, including a dynamic rendition of *All the whores like the way I ride* (better known by its expurgated title *The girls go crazy about the way I walk!*) on which Bunk drives the lead with fierce vigour. Russell mentioned *I'm making believe* as his favourite recording made by the band that year, but it has not seen the light of day since.

Of the titles recorded on the following evening, the earlier ones seem not to have been good enough to issue; three of the sides that were put out were features for Bunk's sidemen. Baby Dodds was on the wagon on account of his health, but somebody sneaked a bottle into the session and he had a drop. This made him feel like singing, and his wooden vocal on *Listen to me* is grafted onto Bunk's standard blues theme, with the trumpeter playing in a coarse and inaccurate way. Lewis plays the traditional chorus on *High Society* in an undemonstrative manner, probably inhibited from expressing himself fully by the poor form of his leader, whose work on *Shine* is all over the place; we may deduce that Bunk had been on one of his bar-crawls that day. Finally, the bass player was given the limelight on a long version of *Slow Drag's Boogie Woogie*, demonstrating admirably the power and drive of his playing.

Recording activity seems to have gone on for most of the next day and evening. First Lewis made three fine titles with the rhythm section. Bunk then entered to add his accompaniment for a local character, Ed 'Noon' Johnson, a street singer who played the bazooka (made from a stove-pipe) – though not on the recording of *Noon's Blues*. His relaxed, colourful voice is also heard in novelty vein on *The cat's got kittens*, made after Jim Robinson arrived. Bunk had his playing under control, although his attack was not particularly crisp; perhaps he was standing too near the microphone.

Some successful band sides were made before Bunk and George gave way to 'Wooden' Joe Nicholas and Albert Burbank, who recorded with the remainder of the group under the title of the Original Creole Stompers. During rehearsal, George's wife Jeanette was afraid that Wooden Joe would blow the walls off his house, but both he and Bunk said that he was not as powerful as his idol, Buddy Bolden. He was there to make new versions of titles from his previous session without the echo. The band started out with Jim Robinson on trombone, but *St Louis Blues* was to feature the legendary Joe Petit, Buddy's step-father. He was 70 years old, almost completely deaf and without teeth. Having made his considerable reputation playing valve trombone he now took over Jim's slide instrument; he had not played for several years, but he was terribly excited by the chance to record. On the first take he was all over the place, even in the wrong key at times, but the next time round he performed in an incredibly forceful, if basic, way. He was doing so well by that time that he stayed on for new versions of *Eh la bas* and *Up jumped the devil*; when the latter was issued on American Music with Robinson listed as the trombonist, few people suspected the mistake. Bunk rounded off the session with two more successful titles, and also a number that were rejected.

Bill Russell had a long-standing plan to record a New Orleans brass band for the first time, and the moment seemed propitious. It was to be based, understandably, on Bunk Johnson's band, with instruments added in an attempt to obtain the authentic sound. Kid Shots Madison was to play second trumpet, Isidore Barbarin and Adolphe Alexander of the Onward Brass Band were to play alto and baritone horns respectively, and Joseph 'Red' Clark, manager of the Eureka, tuba. Dodds took the snare drum, handing his bass drum to Marrero. Russell was prepared to hire some musicians to play saxophones, standard in New Orleans brass bands at that time

Kid Shots Madison with Bunk while in Bunk's Brass Band

and since, but his regular players were against this, saying that they would muddy the sound.

In the event, Russell's ambition seemed as if it would be thwarted by Bunk's celebrations of the previous evening. Russell and Williams went along to keep an eye on him but gave up in exhaustion at 4 a.m. At that point they were at a saloon called the Pig Pen, where Alphonse Picou had a band, and when the musicians packed up, the pianist, Sadie Crosby, invited them all back to her place for a party. Bunk, needless to say, decided to go, while the others went home to snatch some sleep. Russell had more or less given up the idea of recording that day, but Bunk returned at 7.30 and by mid-day, when Russell went to look for him, was out in the yard polishing his trumpet for the session.

The music recorded is not a complete representation of a New Orleans brass band, lacking as it does the full weight of sound. The addition of another trumpet and trombone and the use of a large parade-style bass drum in place of Dodds's dance-band model would probably have made all the difference. Nevertheless some very enjoyable and often moving music was made, with the trumpets combining well and the higher pitch of Lewis's E flat clarinet enabling him to sing out over the band. To collectors who had never heard the traditional funeral hymns and such numbers as *Oh, didn't he ramble* (which were used to lift the spirits when leaving the cemetery) played in this way, the recordings came as very fresh and exciting indeed. It is possible to argue that Russell would have done better to record one of the working brass bands – the Onward, the Eureka or John Casimir's Young Tuxedo – intact but as it turned out had plenty of opportunities to do so later.

John Casimir's brass band. John Casimir recorded with his Young Tuxedo Brass Band in 1958

Bunk's Brass Band was a step in the right direction as well as a valuable documentation of the trumpeter's own approach to such work.

After the session, Shots, tired from five hours of recording, asked Bunk if he would take his place in the Pig Pen band. Bunk was glad to. He did not know, however, that, it being a Friday night, the job went on until seven o'clock next morning. Apparently he got through the small hours without trouble, and then played at a Saturday night dance in the country. Russell was astonished by Bunk's stamina and enthusiasm; playing, when he was enjoying it, never seemed to tire him at all. But he could be very tiring for the people around him, as future events in a much larger metropolis were to prove. Russell and Williams, among others, felt that Bunk's music had a good chance, if exposed to a wider audience, of supplanting swing and 'businessman's bounce' in the popular mind. The time seemed ripe to put this to the test.

CHAPTER 10

THE STUYVESANT CASINO

Eugene Williams was particularly determined to promote Bunk Johnson with his band in New York. He had inherited some money and had a large enough apartment to accommodate the whole band. The musicians were put in readiness to move to the North and to stay there for up to a year if the venture was successful. Most of them had never been outside Louisiana, but it was hoped, if homesickness set in, that in due course they would be able to bring their families to join them. In the meantime Williams was scouring New York for a suitable venue; he had intended the band to play at a smart nightclub or restaurant but, understandably, no such establishment was willing to take a risk with such an unknown quantity. Russell eventually found a place in what was then the Jewish quarter on Second Avenue that had a large ballroom and a management prepared to let it out for a reasonable monthly sum. Shabby and away from the centre of things, it was nevertheless the best that they could get.

It had been decided that the band should have a pianist for the trip, and George Lewis was given the job of finding one. He tried to get Charlie Hamilton, but he already had a steady job. The final choice was a younger man, Alton Purnell, brother of the saxophonist Theodore Purnell who had taken part in a notable New Orleans recording session with Lee Collins in 1929. Alton had worked with Isaiah Morgan, Alphonse Picou and Big Eye, and, in the 1930s in Sidney Desvigne's big band. He was an admirer of Earl Hines and of the New Orleans cabaret pianist Walter 'Fats' Pichon, and had recently been working as accompanist to the singer Pleasant 'Cousin Joe' Joseph at the Famous Door on Bourbon Street. He seems an unlikely choice; Lewis picked him because he played mostly chords, and – musically, at least – events were to prove him triumphantly right in his judgement. Baby Dodds, back in Chicago, was willing to join them in New York; surprisingly, his

Poster announcing the appearance of Bunk Johnson's band at the Stuyvesant Casino at the end of 1945

BUNK JOHNSON
AND HIS NEW ORLEANS BAND

Featuring:

GEORGE LEWIS	**BABY DODDS**
JIM ROBINSON	**SLOW DRAG**
LAWRENCE MARRERO	**ALTON PURNELL**

●

DANCING
Every Night Except Monday

From 9:00 P. M. to 1:00 A. M.

●

STUYVESANT CASINO
140 Second Ave. (near 9th St.) New York City

Two Blocks East of Wanamaker's—Easily reached by all main subway, "L" and bus lines. From West Side lines, take 8th Street crosstown bus to Second Ave.

ADMISSION: $1.00 including Federal tax

 345

distinguished career had never taken him there before.

The members of the band caught the train north on Monday 24th September, but Bunk, in his time-honoured manner, was not among them. Jeanette Lewis was left with the job of searching for him. When the others arrived, they found the pace and way of life in New York bewildering. Bunk arrived on the following day and Russell took him to the local union to obtain clearance for the band to work in New York. At first this proved almost impossible, but when Bunk exercised his silver tongue on one of the officials the permit was signed. The band's residency at the Stuyvesant Casino started next day on schedule, but Williams was probably determined enough for them to play in New York to have defied the union, if necessary.

Even before the band played before the public, discord between Bunk and the others made itself apparent, Bunk wanted to play the current hit songs, and thought that the group should have a repertoire large enough to perform for a month without repeating a tune. This confounded Lewis and his friends, who were accustomed to making do with a very limited range of numbers. Purnell intimated that Fats Pichon was a better musician than Bunk, and that even he did not know that many tunes. Bunk got back at Purnell, who was playing from piano arrangements, by changing keys so that the pianist had to transpose; when Purnell objected, Bunk offered to give him music lessons. A scene also ensued when the others wanted to play a tune in a different key to the one Bunk chose, and while he was out of the room they proved to their own satisfaction that it sounded better that way. Bunk came back and accused Lewis of trying to take over the band. After that Lewis decided to go home. He went and sat alone in a park near Williams's apartment; Russell found him there and, convinced that his going would break up the whole band, managed to persuade him to stay. George was not the sort to let his friends down, and clearly he felt a lot of gratitude to Russell and Williams, but he must have been pretty desperate with Bunk at that time.

The band played in public for the first time on the Friday. The Casino was crowded with 400 enthusiasts, among them many musicians, and most were very excited by what they heard. For a while all was harmony, musically speaking at least, although the members of the band were very puzzled by the fact that the audience sat and listened rather than dancing; in their home surroundings appreciation of the playing was expressed in movement by the dancers, not by passive intellectual absorption, and they thought that they must be doing something wrong. Comments by those who heard them show that, however motionless their response may have been, the people in the audience were experiencing a vitality and colour, a sheer naturalness in the music, that was like nothing they had heard before. From this communal exposure to such a direct celebration of the life force grew up a whole new movement towards 'purity' in jazz, expanding on the romance expressed in *Jazzmen*. In the long run a good deal of damage was done, even to Bunk's own cause, by such over-reaction, but we must accept at least that the music that gave motivation to such a crusade was of tremendous appeal. It expressed a freedom from neurosis and artificiality that made a great impact on the sort of intellectuals and middle-class college students who made up the bulk of its subsequent following. There was at the time, in artistic circles, a disillusion with the material values of American society, forcefully expressed in Henry Miller's book *The Air-conditioned Nightmare* – which, incidentally, contains a chapter about Weeks Hall and his home, The Shadows.

The theorising of the enthusiasts made little sense to the musicians, but their appreciation was sincere if rather high-flown. Unfortunately these enthusiasts could not come to the Stuyvesant Casino every evening, much as they would have liked to, and after the successful opening business slowed down to the extent that the band was moved to a smaller hall within the same building. Despite this set-back, the musicians were playing well, with Bunk's lip in better shape than it had been since his rediscovery; this, in itself, may have been a spur to his growing ambition. He kept trying material that was unfamiliar to the others and would force them through it by sheer domination. He considered himself very much the boss and the star attraction. He never stood up to play, and Lewis and Robinson were compelled to remain seated during their solos because he could not abide their overshadowing him; he would take his trumpet and break into their solos when they did. Although the audience was probably unaware of these problems, they made Lewis and the others feel that they could not give of their best.

After a while, thanks to a good deal of publicity in the press, the audiences picked up and the band was able to go back into the big hall. The disruptive forces, however, were gathering strength. Bunk expressly forbade the others to take part in any activities outside the band, although he does not seem to have seen this restriction as applying to himself.

Baby Dodds, at least, was in demand to sit in with Muggsy Spanier at Nick's and also at Eddie Condon's club. A superb drummer, he naturally attracted a good deal of attention at the Casino from aspiring percussionists. He was also quite a showman, and all the admiration he received went to his head and caused him to put on a crowd-pleasing display; this, as well as being inappropriate for the sort of band he was in, took the spotlight away from Bunk. The trumpeter would respond by changing the

tempo in the middle of a tune and generally needling Dodds. Eventually, Dodds got so fed up with it that he turned up one evening too drunk to play properly. Bunk capped this with a bender of his own, and threatened to walk out on the band if Dodds stayed in it. It was an ironical situation, where the one member of the band who was fully capable of executing his leader's musical aspirations was also his equal in temperament, and refused to share Bunk's estimate of his own importance. The bad feeling between them lasted for the rest of Bunk's life.

The feeling in the band as a whole was becoming bad. Jim Robinson, whom Bunk had already wanted to replace with Sandy Williams, felt like giving up and going home. Lewis, who was having trouble with his teeth, started to drink heavily enough to make himself ill. Bill Russell kept patching things up, but their music was deteriorating. Bunk would often fall asleep on the stand; on one occasion Wild Bill Davison, who was in the crowd, filled the gap left by the dozing leader. Davison was a forceful trumpeter, but nothing he played could disturb the defaulter's repose in his nearby chair. By this time Bunk was referring to his partners as 'emergency musicians'; it is doubtful whether he ever really considered them as partners, or the band as his band, although he seems to have been quite content to play with them up to the time of the New York excursion.

Ironically, just as the band was falling apart as a valid musical unit, the takings at the Casino were beginning to reduce Gene Williams's losses and the major companies were asking the musicians to record. They made four titles for Decca in November 1945 and took part in two sessions producing four sides each for Victor in December. The Decca titles are the better because of superior recording and because Lewis had all his top teeth taken out during the intervening period (Albert Nicholas substituted for him at the Casino). The relative merits of the recordings for American Music and these in New York have often been discussed, usually to the detriment of the latter. Probably owing to the disturbances at the Casino, they do not have the same feeling of co-operative vitality as do their predecessors, but there are compensations. A particular pleasure on the Decca sides is Baby Dodds's drumming, an outstanding example being heard on *Alexander's Ragtime Band*. Best of all is *Tishomingo Blues*, a beautiful tune given an outstanding performance, with Bunk's forthright trumpet leading the way.

The Victor company, which should have known better, contrived to spoil the sound of the band. Baby's bass drum was muffled with a blanket, and the overall effect is nowhere near as crisp as on the Decca recordings. Purnell was also given a dreadful piano, though it was probably no worse than the one at the Casino.

Baby Dodds

93

Despite this impediment Purnell proves to be the ideal band pianist: solid, reliable and warm-hearted. Lewis's clarinet playing understandably has a hollow sound and rather lacks confidence; Robinson also sounds relatively subdued. Nevertheless, there are some glowing performances, particularly on *One Sweet Letter* and *Sister Kate* from the first session and *Franklin Street Blues*, with a fine solo from Bunk from the second. Despite the vast amount of material recorded by Bunk now available from American Music we should have been much the poorer had these New York sessions not taken place. The results perhaps show the trumpeter moving away from the elemental music of his colleagues, but the divergence is not disruptive, and we have, in a way, the best of both worlds; Bunk rising like a phoenix from the earth of his earlier associations into the spacious firmament of his aspirations.

On New Year's Day 1946 Bunk and the band were featured at a concert at Town Hall, New York. Also on the bill were Clarence Williams with a washboard band and a group led by Henry 'Red' Allen. The Master of Ceremonies was Orson Welles, reading notes in flowery style by Frederic Ramsey Jr, which evidently caused the band some amusement. The musicians accompanied a powerful gospel singer, Sister Ernestine Washington, and shortly afterwards they recorded four titles with her which, originally made for the Jubilee label, were actually issued on Disc. The sound on the recording is poor, with the singer distorted and the band very much in the background, but a good deal of appropriate fervour is generated, with Purnell pounding away in sanctified style. Baby Dodds remembered the session with affection because they all played well; it seems, perhaps in deference to the religious nature of the material, as though animosities were forgotten.

Another recording date in early 1946 saw the band making a V-disc at the Stuyvesant Casino. One Red Jones is on drums, Baby Dodds having gone back to Chicago with his health impaired – probably equally by the aggravation of working with Bunk and by the resultant drinking (which was strictly against his doctor's orders). The mysterious Jones does a workmanlike job on the recordings. Bunk seems to be going his own way, sometimes leaving the band trailing in his wake; he sounds quite perfunctory at times but plays a dynamic and inventive solo on *I can't escape from you* and executes the breaks on *Snag it* with reasonable precision. Lewis sounds uncomfortable with his new false teeth, and in comparison with his best work is just going through the motions. The Casino piano confirms its bad reputation and Purnell must be heartily congratulated for getting any sound out of it at all; he has a nice rolling solo on *Snag it*. The latter is unfortunately faded on the Folklyric issue, which includes these recordings as well as the titles from the Decca and Victor sessions, but the track is heard complete on a NoLa reissue of material first issued on the Purist label.

The band's final performance at the Stuyvesant Casino took place six days after the V-disc recording, on 12th January 1946. Williams is reputed to have lost 3,000 dollars in bringing the musicians to New York and supporting them for four months, despite some popular success after the favourable publicity had taken effect. They returned to New Orleans and most were heartily glad to be home, although with hindsight George Lewis accounted the trip one of the biggest thrills in his musical career. Lewis was plainly unhappy with Bunk's attitude towards the rest of them, but he did not (as did some of the others) sustain any hatred, and remained firm in his admiration for the trumpeter's musicianship and inventiveness. Lewis did reckon, however, that Bunk had a fixation about wanting to emulate the musical authority of the old 'professors' who held their followers in thrall through their legitimate expertise and disciplinary authority. It seems that he felt he should have been able to train the band as James Humphrey might once have done. But he overlooked the fact that his sidemen were already expert and experienced in a field whose conventions suited them admirably, no matter how irksome its limitations may have been to more schooled and ambitious musicians.

Bunk did fulfil his aspirations as a teacher by tutoring a young sailor on the trumpet. At the same time, earnest clarinettists approached Lewis for hints about his playing, but he was not able to put any of it into words. Unlike Bunk's, his artistry was entirely instinctive and transcendental, to the extent that he was able to do what a conventional musician would consider impossible.

Towards the end of the first Stuyvesant Casino engagement, Bill Colburn, who had been involved in the original recordings for Jazz Man and had seen a good deal of Bunk in San Francisco, came to New York. Colburn had been interesting himself in Kid Ory's band, now a regular outfit in Los Angeles. It was a rather more polished group than Bunk's, and made up of men who thoroughly understood each others' styles. The band's recordings from that time show a tendency towards the dixieland style, less unpredictable but lacking the emotional intensity to be found in Bunk's group, though Mutt Carey's trumpet playing is always rewarding. Accounts of the musicians' playing in the flesh indicate an ability to play a wider range of material in an inventive way, very much the sort of thing Bunk was looking for in his band. With this in his mind's ear, Colburn was very disappointed with the New York band, and walked out of a Victor recording session in disgust. It was probably his influence that finally decided Gene Williams that the Stuyvesant Casino group was no longer the proper vehicle for Bunk Johnson's artistry. In any case, on account of the personal

Overleaf
The band for Bunk's New York engagement at the beginning of 1946: Kaiser Marshall (drums), Slow Drag Pavageau (double bass), Jim Robinson (trombone), Bunk (trumpet), Don Ewell (piano) and George Lewis (clarinet)

95

problems between Bunk and the others, the writing was clearly on the wall.

Ironically, by the time the residency was terminated the proprietor of the Stuyvesant, Benjamin Menshell, was convinced that the band was potentially a popular success and asked Bunk to come back to New York with his band. Williams had gone off to California, following up Colburn's glowing reports about Ory, so Bunk had to negotiate with Menshell, who was convinced that the band would be successful only if Lewis and Robinson were in it. Bunk managed to persuade him to do without Purnell and Dodds. A young white admirer of Jelly Roll Morton, Don Ewell, was brought in on piano. Bunk wanted George Thompson, the drummer who had played in the Boston band, but he was not available, and Kaiser Marshall, who had spent many years in Fletcher Henderson's distinguished New York orchestra, was brought in. Marshall, however, was drinking heavily, could not keep time and was a total wash-out as far as the band was concerned. His replacement, Alphonse Steele, had recorded with Red Allen and Billie Holiday during the 1930s. Although Russell recalled that he had some difficulty adapting to a smaller group than he was used to, Steele seems to have fitted in well.

Predictably, this second New York trip was even more trying for the musicians than the first. Lawrence Marrero was not wanted by the Stuyvesant management, probably on the basis that the band led by Art Hodes, which had played there in the meantime, used only six men, and they did not see why they should pay for an extra one. When Marrero found out that he was not to go, he was very angry with Lewis, but the decision had nothing to do with the clarinettist.

Even before the musicians set out, Bunk was up to his individual tricks again. On the night before they were to leave he was showing the tickets that Mr Menshell had sent him to all his friends at the Coliseum Arena. When they were ready to go Bunk was nowhere to be found; hard though they searched, Lewis, Robinson and Slow Drag had not located him by the Sunday night before they were due to open in New York. Lewis had to telephone Mr Menshell and explain how things stood. Bunk turned up at Robinson's house late that night and fell asleep in a chair. In the morning Pearl, Jim's wife, had to retrieve his trumpet and his camel-hair coat from the bar where he had traded them for a continued supply of drinks.

The best they could do was catch a slow train on the Monday night, and they arrived too late to work on the following evening. Art Hodes continued to fill in; Bunk thought that this would give him the opportunity to spend a night on the town, but the management would not let him out of their sight. His frustration was no doubt assuaged by the fact that since his last visit the Casino had obtained a spirits licence, but the incident put him in a bad mood and, according to Lewis, set the tone of the five weeks the band spent at the Stuyvesant. Despite this, the notable lack of Marrero, and even, at the outset, Marshall's errant drumming, most of the enthusiasts who came to the Casino during that second visit seem to have loved the music as much as ever. On at least one occasion the famous and notorious negro folk-singer Leadbelly (Huddie Ledbetter) sat in with the band. The management even brought Bunk's wife Maude up to New York, no doubt thinking that she would be a stabilising influence on him, but it is not clear whether this was the case.

Bill Russell organised one recording session in New York during the band's stay, but it featured only Bunk, Don Ewell and Alphonse Steele. It finds the trumpeter in mellow form, able to spread his ideas in this sparer line-up with no shortage of invention. Ewell's Morton-inspired piano playing is expertly supportive as well as being an effective voice in its own right, and Steele keeps the rhythm going in an undemonstrative manner. The tunes – ballads, vaudeville standards and such like – are by no means typical of the New Orleans tradition. The only out-and-out jazz number is *Ja da*, but Bunk takes all this assorted material in his stride, and, although lovers of the New Orleans sound were rather taken aback when the recordings were issued, it was a very rewarding session. The results show just how flexible and subtle Bunk's playing could be when he felt in tune with his material and master of the situation.

The band's engagement lasted until 31st May, when Bunk's association with George Lewis ended for good. The trumpeter probably felt little emotion about their parting of the ways, but Lewis, although doubtless relieved that all the personal strife was over, was well aware that he owed to Bunk the opportunity to transcend his obscure part-time career in New Orleans and move, however briefly, into the limelight. While in New York his playing had been admired enough for him never to be entirely forgotten again. Ironically, in the long run the homely clarinettist was to achieve the success that eluded the ambitious and sophisticated trumpeter.

CHAPTER 11

THE LAST TESTAMENT

Bunk Johnson had evidently formed a close friendship with Don Ewell. His life from this time on may be charted, albeit intermittently, from the letters that he sent to Ewell from New Iberia during the periods when he was at home. These show that he was always keen to work with Ewell, continually trying to use him to set up engagements in the North as well as to help him obtain money that he considered was owing to him for the jobs he did do. Bunk's correspondence was convoluted by the fact that the pianist was not always easy to locate. Ewell was often in hospital suffering from spells of nervous depression, and, when he was well, he would work wherever his playing was in demand.

We are fortunate that this correspondence, which survives only in the letters received by Ewell and not those he himself wrote, has been made available in *Footnote* magazine. It contains some very personal details in Bunk's response to the pianist's mental problems, and has been published only since his death. The letters are invaluable since they fill the gaps between other published information and because they offer a rare and direct glimpse of Bunk's attitude to life, his musical ideals and his estimation of his own importance. His personality is exuberantly embodied through the medium of his portable Corona typewriter; despite a unique attitude to spelling and punctuation that renders all his compositions into colloquial patterns, the correspondence leaves no doubt about his intelligence and articulateness.

In total, the letters are harrowing and saddening. They show the man's ebullient optimism and uncompromising egotism slowly deteriorating into a plaintive disappointment in those who, he considered, let him down. He remains ingratiating about the friends who stayed faithful to his cause, and is particularly concerned to encourage Ewell to maintain a positive attitude to life through his problems, the better to fulfil himself as a musician.

Knowing something about Bunk's mental make-up, we can consider that his feelings of friendship were more overtly self-centred than is usual in civilised society, while over any questions of money owing to him, we must remember that he was a spendthrift who did not count the cost of the liquor that the promoters of his jobs had (or believed they had) to pour into him as deductable from his emoluments. Nor did he feel any obligation, unless all the arrangements were absolutely to his liking, to provide value for money in terms of availability or performance. It is perhaps ironic that in his letters to Ewell, Bunk is continually urging him to moderate his drinking for the sake of his health; but until the end, thanks to his exceptionally strong constitution, Bunk's own health does not seem to have been affected in any long-term way by his alcoholic indulgence, and the professional lapses that it often caused could be rationalised as no more than was deserved by those who upset him.

From the letters, we can tell that Bunk was still expecting a call from Mr Menshell for a further residency at the Stuyvesant Casino in the autumn of 1946. It transpired, however, that the manager still wanted Lewis, Robinson and Pavageau and did not want Ewell. Bunk wrote and told him to forget the deal, saying that he would soon find out who was the main attraction if he went ahead without him, and it seems that Menshell then lost interest in bringing any band up from the South. Bunk, in the meantime, had another offer – to appear at a concert at Orchestra Hall in Chicago organised by John T. Schenk, who asked him to name the musicians with whom he wanted to play. Ewell was to be the pianist, but, apart from Baby Dodds (whom Bunk was adamant he did not want), he did not know any Chicago musicians. Schenk picked Preston Jackson on trombone, Darnell Howard on clarinet, John Lindsey on bass and Clifford 'Snags' Jones on drums. Snags, thus named because he had a gap in his front teeth, does seem to have been known to Bunk from the past, and it is likely that he was the mysterious Red Jones who replaced Baby Dodds at the Stuyvesant.

The Orchestra Hall concert was not a success, at least as far as Bunk's performance was concerned. Also featured were the fine and versatile guitarist and singer Lonnie Johnson, who may well, as he often did in Chicago at that time, have sat in with the band, and the Jimmy Yancey Trio, which teamed the great pianist with his wife Estelle 'Mama' Yancey, an exceptionally powerful, earthy survivor of the classic blues tradition. Bunk seems to have believed that Baby Dodds was to be presented as a solo attraction, as he was at the earlier New York Town Hall concert; this may have come from the appearance in the printed programme of an advertisement for a set of Dodds's drum recordings, for Dodds

Lee Collins, Southland Studio, 1953

himself is not mentioned as being among those taking part. This was not a very diplomatic response on the part of the organisers to Bunk's quite open dislike of the drummer; in the event, the disgusted trumpeter turned up two hours late for the concert, and, when he did arrive, played very badly. He may have been drunk, but considering his tendencies it may equally have been a coldly deliberate rebuke.

Some of the audience at the concert were so in thrall to Bunk's reputation that they were not too disappointed, but those who were looking for fault in the whole Bunk Johnson parade needed no further convincing that he should have stayed in Louisiana, and he probably did his cause no good with other promoters who might have booked him. Nevertheless, a young enthusiast called Harold Drob, who was returning to New York from California after investigating, and admiring, Kid Ory's music, attended the concert and was convinced, by the way that the band of expert and sympathetic musicians backed Bunk, that this was the sort of group with which he should be playing regularly.

Bunk spent some time in Chicago with Don Ewell, and the two men worked together wherever they could. Jack Stanley heard them sitting in with Lee Collins's band at the Victory Club on North Clark Street, a rough saloon with a basic clientele of whores and labourers which Collins was turning into an unlikely mecca for jazz enthusiasts. The sound of the two trumpeters playing together with Ewell and the drummer Jerome 'Pork Chops' Smith was an unforgettable experience, and Stanley was delighted to learn, in the spring of 1947, that Bunk was once again in Chicago. He arranged for him and Ewell to play with Doc Evans's band in a concert at the University of Minnesota.

A previous letter from New Iberia indicates that John Schenk was intending to organise another Chicago concert in April, but it is not clear whether this took place. Bunk was evidently hoping to play with the band from the previous concert, but had learnt that Snags had died in the meantime. The drummer had taken part in a Victor recording date in a band organised by his old New Orleans school friend Preston Jackson, and he did not live long enough to see the results issued. The group's trumpet player, Louis Ogletree, is not ideal for the style, and it is tantalising to think that, had Bunk been in Chicago at the time, he might have been chosen instead.

While in Chicago for the concert, Bunk hoped for some other irregular jobs, although he knew that the union would bar him from any steady work. The Minnesota concert, at any rate, was a success, with Bunk on his best behaviour. (The music has been issued on the New Orleans label and shows Bunk blowing strongly and purposefully, nicely offset by the gentler, Bix Beiderbecke-inspired cornet of Doc Evans, with the rest of the band in enthusiastic, if not very subtle, support.) As guest of honour, Bunk received a great reception and was interviewed on stage by Jack Stanley. The good old story was trotted out in a most affable manner, but it is interesting to note that the number of Bunk's children had increased from 12 to 14 since a previous interview – the latter being his usual figure for the family roster of his own generation. The number, twice repeated, cannot have been a random slip and is more likely to be an example of his very approximate respect for the truth. On the same morning he had lectured on jazz history to Professor Tremaine McDowell's classes in American Studies, and no doubt he found the earnest academic scene a source of cynical amusement.

Schenk's plans for Bunk included a tour through the midwestern states, playing dances and concerts on Sundays. There is no indication in Bunk's letters of how many of these took place, but the considerable amount of money he subsequently believed he was owed by Schenk (800 dollars) seems to show that there were quite a few. This money was beginning to occupy his mind a good deal by the time he was back in New Iberia in July, for, to the disappointment of his wife and daughter, he had returned flat broke and he had debts at home; he said that three months 'fooling with John Schenk' in Chicago had actually cost him money. He had also left some belongings behind and was looking for Don's help in getting them back. He was grateful to David Bell, who put him up while he was in Chicago.

Another account, from Catherine Jacobson (who was involved in the first, and apparently only, Orchestra Hall concert) of Bunk's dealings with Schenk and Bell shows that he was continually coming up with tales of being robbed, getting money from them, and that he left *them* flat broke. He still managed to charm them, however.

Bunk was still looking for work, having been negotiating with a man in San Francisco for a regular job. Eugene Williams was there already, promoting a dance hall to feature Ory's band. Bunk was concerned to keep his plans secret from Williams, presumably in case he spread the word about how difficult an employee the trumpeter could be. Williams had, in fact, tried to raise the money to enable Bunk to play with a band of his own choosing after the end of the Stuyvesant Casino engagement, but Harold Drob had no confidence in Gene's financial acumen – rightly, as it turned out, for the Ory venture was not a success.

In the autumn of 1947 Bob Maltz founded the New York Jazz Club and promoted a series of concerts and dances. Bunk Johnson took part in what was probably the inaugural concert, on 6th September. With him in the band were Jimmy Archey on trombone, the New Orleans clarinettists Edmond Hall and Omer Simeon, Danny Barker on guitar, Cyrus St Clair on tuba and Freddie Moore on drums. Bunk had hoped that Don Ewell would be on piano, but in the event his place was taken by another young white stylist, Ralph Sutton. Leadbelly was also on the programme. An obviously amateur recording, suffering from distortion and variable speed, was made of the proceedings. The production was evidently a bit of a shambles, with the Master of Ceremonies (presumably Maltz himself) only barely in control of the musicians. Where the recording allows, there is some good music to be heard, but Bunk himself sounds tentative, inaccurate and rather disinterested. Perhaps his sub-standard playing can be excused on this occasion, because he may be heard explaining that he had arrived by plane from New Orleans only two hours earlier and had not eaten for over 24 hours. The results, such as they are, were issued on the Rarities label.

Bunk Johnson's return to New York enabled Harold Drob to put into practice his desire to enable the trumpeter to play in a band of his own choosing. He got to know Bunk as well as he could, and came to admire him as a man as well as a musician, particularly for his vitality and his sense of humour. He tended, perhaps, to over-compensate, entirely taking Bunk's side against his earlier associates. As has been shown, Bunk could be exceptionally charming and ingratiating, and he was very capable of presenting his musical ideals reasonably to a sympathetic hearer; also, like many an egotist, he was very exhilarating company as long as he was allowed his head. Drob let Bunk follow his principle that the band should play for dancing and must be made up of musicians who could read well and who were prepared to rehearse thoroughly. He wanted a repertoire with as much variety as possible and was particularly keen to play ragtime, which he felt was due for a comeback and which needed expert musicianship and strict discipline to bring off properly.

Bunk wanted to play at the Stuyvesant Casino again, so Drob booked the hall initially for a Friday and Saturday evening, 7th and 8th November. The band that Bunk picked included Alphonse Steele on drums and Danny Barker, who had been in the band at the New York Jazz Club concert, on guitar. Barker was from New Orleans and was the nephew of Paul Barbarin; he had recently left the big band of the celebrated entertainer Cab Calloway. Clarinettist Garvin Bushell, trombonist Ed Cuffee and bassist Wellman Braud (originally Breaux, a Cajun name) had all worked in big bands during the 1930s. All were expert readers and accustomed to the discipline of complex arrangements, but they were still capable of expressing themselves appropriately in the context of a small group. The original pianist was Bunk's old partner from Kansas City, the Texan Sammy Price, but he soon dropped out in favour of the gifted pianist and arranger Don Kirkpatrick. Bunk may have come across Bushell and Cuffee in the Clarence Williams group that played at the 1946 New Year concert; in any case, he had heard enough of them to know that they could do what he wanted. They were accomplished without being individualists, willing to work for the good of the band.

Bunk led his band by example. On the musicians' first night together he set out to prove that he was the equal of any one of them, and gained their whole-hearted respect. The hall was booked for five more nights over a two-week period, and towards the end of that time the band was playing to Bunk's satisfaction, which by no means demanded a subjugation of the other musicians' stylistic contributions. An amateur recording made on the second night shows the band tackling a variety of popular dance material with discipline, understanding and no lack of verve. Bunk is playing with drive and subtlety, much as he always did when on his best form; he contributes confident and logical solos and an authoritative lead, and shows an even more searching variation of phrasing than usual. It is a pity that the recording, issued on the NoLa label, is sub-standard and allows only a shadow of the music's physical presence, but no assessment of the trumpeter's talent is complete without it.

Despite the satisfactory musical growth of the group, the dances did not attract enough public attention to prevent a steady drain on Harold Drob's resources. Enthusiasts who had raved about the earlier Stuyvesant band were disappointed by the less earthy sound and by the absence of George Lewis and Jim Robinson, for although Bunk's new recruits were all experienced musicians, they did not have popular reputations such as to draw the less committed New York fans. In addition, in order to keep the band together Drob rather exposed them to the market, thinning the audience for each performance still further. He had to terminate the dances, but he felt that, were Bunk to appear on recordings with a band that played as he wanted, a promoter might be persuaded to hire him. He offered the trumpeter *carte blanche* to record 12 tunes, taking up an offer of financial assistance for such a project from his friend Bill Stendahl.

Bunk was staying with Bill Loughborough, who, along with John Schenk and Bill Page, had been heavily involved in the ill-fated Chicago concert. He and Page, however, seem not to have been caught up in the financial recriminations that soured Bunk's feelings for Schenk. Loughborough had some experience of recording and suggested that they use the Carnegie Recital Hall because of its excellent acoustics, and they all agreed that only one microphone should be used. Bunk was particularly insistent about this, since he felt that multiple microphones would distort the rhythm and the relationships between the instruments – another example of his practical sophistication.

Although Drob was prepared for Bunk to pick an entirely new band if he wanted, he felt that it was only fair that his existing group should have the chance to make the recordings. Danny Barker could not be found in time for the rehearsals but Bunk was confident of his ability to fit in when the time came. Bunk wanted to make a selection of arrangements from the *Red Back Book of Quality Rags* as well as some tunes that had sounded good at the dances. The rags were to be played as written, but Bunk was not entirely rigid about this; he welcomed suggestions for improvements compatible with the overall structure, and admitted he was making adjustments that he felt to be appropriate in his own part. The other tunes were to be played as head arrangements, with only the sequence of ensemble choruses and solos worked out in advance.

Among the rags they tried was *Kinklets*, a complicated piece which Bushell jokingly suggested Bunk would be unable to manage; in response, Bunk took the clarinet part and played it on the trumpet. Drob felt that they would probably not have recorded the tune had this not happened, and, indeed they had some trouble in finding the right tempo for it. The recordings were made on three days at the end of December 1947. Drob hired a portable Presto machine and received instruction in its use from Loughborough, whose job would not allow him to be present. The recording level was set up at the outset and left unchanged throughout. The resulting sound, if not brilliantly lifelike, was as clean a representation of Bunk Johnson's tone as was ever achieved, and its slightly clinical ambience was in keeping with the music.

Although, when they were eventually issued, the recordings gave collectors who were in love with the American Music sound a considerable shock, there was nothing revolutionary about them apart from the view of Bunk Johnson that they projected; this was as close to his own view of his artistry as they were ever likely to hear. Some years on they actually sound more old-fashioned, though less rugged, than his previous recordings. They have a turn-of-the-century flavour, with Bunk proving that the rags, played close to the written notes, are hot music in their own right and need only a little extra emphasis from the trumpet to enhance this quality. The ballads also have great charm, played as they are with precision in accordance with Bunk's tenets. This music is most rewarding, although lacking the emotional appeal of the more haphazard repertoire he played with George Lewis and company, and it is valuable because it tells us more about Bunk's place in history. It shows quite clearly that he was a fine bandmaster who could organise a group of musicians to play compatibly in an integrated manner that was entirely suitable for both listening and dancing too. It also shows that his style and musical credo pre-dated jazz as we generally understand it.

Bunk Johnson epitomises a period in New Orleans music when the personal, emotional aspects that we associate with jazz had not yet developed. Buddy Bolden's force was expressed in entirely musical, if instrumentally illegitimate, terms, and the Creoles played the music as written with a fierce, impersonal joy. Bunk was by no means a 'straight' musician, nor was he an illegitimate one; he was able to build on both strains, and to find a middle way, by original application of purely musical effects. This perhaps explains why, although he was as influential as any trumpet player of the early years and much admired by his fellow musicians, he did not have the magnetism to claim Bolden's title of 'King'. Bunk was both ahead of his time and reactionary, the link between the old and the new order, at a time when change was occurring so fast as to make his approach a transitional one.

Baby Dodds, when he met him again in the 1940s, said that Bunk's playing was smoother and more technical than it had been in the old Eagle days. As might have been expected with such a man, he had honed his style and enlarged his store of variational effects over the years of public playing and solitary practice. His basic approach, however, and his understanding of its function in a band, probably changed little. It is significant that he could reveal emotion in his playing only by performing well when he was happy and badly when he was upset. The ability to include these expressions into the content of the music seems to have come only with slightly later musicians, some of whom he influenced. His choice of musicians for his last band was an apt one since big-band swing, in which they were versed, was a return to music expressive through corporate competence and musicianship, untainted by such personal elements as the blues. Bunk's view of the blues was that it was just another tune, to be played perhaps once during an evening; it is significant that, when he came to record as he wished, he steered clear of the medium. However, he could prove that the blues was effective as a purely musical form, and it is fortunate that he was allowed, or persuaded, to include a number of variations on that theme in his earlier recordings.

Ironically, the sessions intended to point Bunk Johnson's way to further work in the North were the cause of his returning home to the South. The weather on the days when the band recorded was exceptionally cold, and culminated in a blizzard. When the musicians left the hall on the final occasion Bunk was aghast at the amount of snow, saying over and over again, 'I left Louisiana for this! Oh no, oh no!' He went home a week later. It had been intended to aim the recordings at the general public through juke-boxes, but they remained unissued until 1952, when George Avakian of Columbia Records organised an LP containing all 12 titles; by that time it was too late to be of benefit to their prime contributor.

Back in New Iberia, Bunk continued, through Harold Drob and Don Ewell, to try to find work in the North. He asked Drob to sound out the members of his 'Local 802 Band', as he called it, on whether they would work with him on a prospective engagement at the Ball of Fire Club in Chicago. All but Bushell, who had a teaching commitment, were willing, but the job never materialised. In September 1948 Bunk was asking Ewell to approach the owner of the Blinking Pup nightclub, on North Clark Street, about a job for a trio or quartet. At the same time he was demonstrating his penury by asking Don to send him a new ribbon for his typewriter. He was 'way down in everything', but was optimistic about being 'Bunk Johnson again in life.' He was still chasing John Schenk for money, without success, and had no job.

Weeks Hall gave Bunk some support, providing liquid refreshment in return for reminiscence and trumpet playing, and his favourite Bull Durham tobacco. Weeks, who also had to bail him out of jail on occasions, never had any illusions about Bunk's reliability. The trumpeter told him that during his period of success he had banked 100,000 dollars and then touched him for five dollars so that he could go and drink at the Hall and Grill and Social Club in New Iberia. On another occasion *Life* magazine wanted to get in touch with Bunk, and contacted Weeks, who told the reporters where to find him. When Bunk answered the phone at the club he was incoherent, just as Hall knew he would be. Weeks gave him the fare to New Orleans to meet the *Life* people, but he never turned up. In August 1948 Bunk wrote a note to Weeks asking for a present of a bicycle for his 'recent' birthday (actually in December!) to enable him to get into town. He even furnished a catalogue for Hall's convenience.

Bunk's letters to Don Ewell became more despondent as 1948 wore on. Then in November a handwritten note came from Maude Johnson, saying that Bunk had had an attack and fallen over; the doctor said it was due to his blood pressure. He was unconscious for two-and-a-half hours and lost his speech. Ewell evidently sent some money, for Maude wrote thanking him and saying that Bunk was much improved and was sitting up in bed. The doctor now said that his eyesight was the cause of his blood pressure, and that a pair of spectacles should cure it! Maude also wrote that she had had a telegram from Chuck Sweningen of *Down Beat* magazine wanting information on Bunk's condition, and asked Ewell to pass her news on to him. Bunk obtained his glasses and his condition improved temporarily, but by the end of November, despite a change of doctor, he was very sick again. On 22nd December he went into hospital for a few days to be given oxygen and came out somewhat better. Maude was very disappointed that Louis Armstrong had not responded to her news, but Bunk was very pleased with all the letters he had been getting and by an article in *Down Beat*.

By March 1949 Bunk seemed to have improved. He was up and around the house, although he could not write because his left arm was useless. Bill Russell had been to see him, and so had Louis Armstrong; the latter explained that he had never received the earlier news, although Maude, probably not knowing how busy he was, thought that he was lying. Maude's next two communications have a tragic irony; a telegram on 2nd July asking for 20 dollars and another on 7th July saying that Bunk was dead. Bill Russell was with him shortly before he died, and Bunk was sitting in a chair, unable to move and scarcely able to talk. Weeks Hall was there around the time he died, and loaned his chauffeur-driven car to take the family to the funeral.

In accordance with his wishes, Maude gave Bunk's trumpet to David Bell, who had helped him in Chicago. He was buried in St Edward's Catholic cemetery in New Iberia and his grave was unmarked for some years. In the late 1970s Bill Russell, from New Orleans, set about organising a headstone, but when Harold Drob visited New Iberia in 1979 it was still not in place; there was only a poorly engraved marker stuck on an adjacent grave. It turned out that the headstone had been completed for some time but that the mason did not know how to find the grave. With Drob's help the stone was taken to the cemetery and set in place. It seems appropriate that the man who helped Bunk Johnson to make his last significant musical gesture in life should also have been the first to honour him properly in death.

CHAPTER 12

THE LEGACY

It is somewhat ironic that the most positive result of Bunk Johnson's renaissance, apart from the immortal recordings he left us, should be one of which he would probably not have approved. The wave of enthusiasm that his recordings, particularly those on the American Music label, aroused, allied with the effect on his faithful admirers of his appearance in the flesh, gave rise to a movement of interest in just those 'emergency musicians' in New Orleans whom he pretended to despise. However, on account of the delay in general circulation of the recordings and the need for the enthusiasts to milk them dry of all meaning and to construct elaborate theories around them, this movement was not immediate. Things went quiet in the Crescent City for a while, but George Lewis kept his band together, using Joe Watkins on drums with either Kid Howard (whose lip was unreliable), Elmer Talbert or Herb Morand on trumpet; for a short while he even employed a young English trumpet player called Ken Colyer, who was one of the most influential figures in the spreading of the New Orleans gospel to Europe. The musicians scuffled for local gigs and found a home at a dance hall called Manny's Tavern, where an increasing number of white enthusiasts came to enjoy their playing.

Bill Russell returned to New Orleans in 1949, partly to see Bunk Johnson during his last illness but also to add to his range of American Music recordings. On 6th July Russell called at George Lewis's home and was told by Jeanette that she thought Bunk must be dead. Slow Drag had had a dream in which Bunk told him to pack his trunk because they were going on a trip; Pavageau had not been feeling well himself and was 'plenty worried'. It was on the next day that Bill learnt officially of Bunk's death, as he was setting out to record 'Wooden' Joe Nicholas in a band including 'Big Eye' Louis Nelson. He also recorded Wooden Joe with Albert Burbank again, and similar groups with Herb Morand and Charlie Love on

Joe Watkins

trumpet. Strangely, he did not record George Lewis's band during that visit.

Other recordings by enthusiasts followed, some of which Russell took over and issued on his own label, featuring such musicians as the trumpeter Kid Thomas Valentine and the clarinettist Emile 'Milé' Barnes. The Lewis band was not excluded; in late 1969 Robert Greenwood, who was acting as a sort of unofficial publicity agent for Lewis, and Herbert Otto recorded the group, with Elmer Talbert, at a party thrown by Otto. The music, some of which has appeared on limited-edition albums, is enjoyably relaxed, and so is that of another group featuring Morand and Burbank caught on the same occasion. Equally excellent formal sessions were recorded in 1950 by Dr Edmond 'Doc' Souchon for Dante Bolletino's Paradox/Pax label and by Good Time Jazz from the West Coast.

The former became known as the *George Lewis Jam Session* and appeared in England on Tempo and Vogue. By this time Alton Purnell, who had not been required at Manny's Tavern, was back in the band.

Earlier in 1950 an event had occurred that was ultimately to project Lewis and his band into a far more widespread fame than they ever achieved under Bunk's leadership. Robert Greenwood persuaded his friend Joseph Roddy, a writer on *Look* magazine, to steer an article he was to write about some New Orleans musicians in the direction of Lewis. The associated photographer was Stanley Kubrick, later to become a famous film director, who was a lover of Lewis's music. The clarinettist, normally taciturn, had a few drinks and made a splendid impression on the two journalists, who all but forgot the original intention to feature the white trumpeter Sharkey Bonano. The article, with some superb photographs by Kubrick, appeared in June 1950. By that time Lewis had gained entry to Bourbon Street, Mecca of the tourists. Passing the El Morocco on their way home from a gig, Lewis and his band were asked to come in and play for the bar staff; the management liked them and they stayed, on and off, for two years. The visitors who heard them there and spread the word around the States, and the widespread distribution of the Good Time Jazz records (which included a splendid version of *Burgundy Street Blues*) added to the publicity of the *Look* article to make Lewis popular far beyond his home town.

During Lewis's time at the El Morocco, the ailing Elmer Talbert was replaced by Herb Morand and then, after Morand's death, by Percy Humphrey. With Humphrey, Lewis appeared in 1951 as a member of the first full New Orleans brass band, the Eureka, to be properly recorded. The clarinettist's spreading popularity was resulting in offers of work in other cities, but he was reluctant to leave home, probably because of his experiences in New York; eventually, however, he agreed to go on tour. Humphrey, who had a steady job as an insurance salesman, would not go with them, so Lewis, not without misgivings, turned again to Kid Howard; he was popular choice on account of his splendid work in the Climax session, but he could not play consistently well any more.

Back at base, however, other trends were appearing. Some recordings by Paul Barbarin's band, doing nicely on Bourbon Street, showed an alternative, less instinctive, approach to New Orleans music-making, while at the other end of the scale an immensely powerful and earthy individualist was making himself felt. Kid Thomas Valentine, son of the instrument-keeper for the brass band at Reserve, Louisiana, was installed at the Moulin Rouge dance hall over in Algiers, where he had been the local popular hero since the 1930s. His own elemental trumpet playing,

the crisp big-band trombone of Louis Nelson (no relation to Big Eye) and the lush but vigorous tenor saxophone of Emanuel Paul gave his band a quite different sound from Lewis's, although the rhythmic principles were much the same. The result was an exciting, if not always calculated, clash of timbres, with the leader pulling the beat all over the place.

Herb Morand and Albert Burbank at a recording session, March 1950

De De Pierce, ably supported by his wife Billie, was reguarly enthusing the dancers at Luthjens. A collection on the Folkways label containing items by Pierces's and Kid Thomas's bands and several others alerted the New Orleans enthusiasts to the fact that the musicians associated with George Lewis were not the only ones still representing the musical traditions of the city. Samuel Charters was responsible for the album, and his book *Jazz: New Orleans, 1885-1963*, detailing the careers of numerous musicians – many of them still active – added to the interest and knowledge.

The early 1960s was a time of great importance in the annals of latter-day New Orleans jazz. Inspired by the music of Bunk and Lewis, and intrigued by Charters' research, with the technical assistance of Bill Russell, Grayson Mills descended on New Orleans to record for his Icon label as many musicians as he could find still playing. At the same time an artist, Larry Borenstein, started informal sessions at his studio, which eventually became properly organised and was called Preservation Hall. From England came a young drummer, Barry Martyn, to study with Cié Frazier and to dig out some of the more obscure musicians (including some not even documented by Charters) to record on his MONO (Music of New Orleans) label. More commercially minded and better equipped technically, the Riverside organisation sent a team to New Orleans to catch the few (as they thought) men left there playing Dixieland music.

Taken together, these recordings present some of the finest New Orleans jazz, mostly using pick-up groups that show how the musicians could combine in a variety of permutations. Notable performances include that by Kid Howard, who made a triumphant comeback, using a cornet in deference to his delicate lip but playing as majestically as his reputation warranted. Kid Thomas performed spectacularly in his uncompromising way both with his own band and in other company. De De Pierce showed himself a superb accompanist of his wife's powerful singing, and the veteran peripatetic Punch Miller, home at last, showed that much of his athletic brilliance was still intact. George Lewis, freed from the cares of touring, proved that he had retained all the old magic, and Albert Burbank equalled him in wizardry. These, and many others, were given the opportunity to parade their talents, and provided a feast of memorable music. Particularly exciting was

Bill Russell (far right) with Eddie Morris

the arrival in the public consciousness of a new New Orleans star. Cap'n John Handy had the reputation of having been the best saxophonist in the city since the 1920s, and now he could be heard more widely. His alto playing was almost unbelievably impressive on a variety of recordings – holding his own with the rampant Kid Howard, blending into a recreation of the old Sam Morgan band and driving with immense momentum on his own.

After that autumnal flowering, recording of New Orleans music, and indeed the music itself in its home surroundings, has inevitably been in gentle decline. Many splendid individual sessions have occurred, and quite a few recordings made earlier by pioneer enthusiasts have made a delayed appearance. The passing of many beloved figures has been partly compensated by the interest in the city's musical tradition of some younger men, often members of a later generation of distinguished families. The brass-band medium in particular, as long as the cooperative spirit is intact, has shown that it can accept a variety of musical attitudes, and luminaries of the city's strong rhythm-and-blues movement, which spawned such popular stars as Fats Domino and Professor Longhair, can play alongside confirmed modernists and such of the elderly men who can still march and make joyful and generally disciplined music. Young, usually white, pilgrims have homed in on New Orleans, found a place in the music and often stayed; these have included many from Europe and even from Japan. Whatever one may think intellectually of these ethnically ambiguous attempts to continue an old and alien tradition, it has to be admitted that they are entirely sincere and tend to thrive in the unique atmosphere of New Orleans, where the heart is as important as the mind in the making of music.

While Bunk Johnson would certainly have looked sideways at the attempts of young men to capture an old sound and to take as their model just those 'emergency musicians' who he felt were capable of playing only in the most basic way, as a teacher, and one who passed his principles on to many younger students, he must have respected their efforts to learn music, especially if these were based on a sound technique and an ability to read. He did not consider his own music a regional attribute, but rather a universally relevant accomplishment. Since he viewed music as important only at the moment of performance, and was not much interested in its permanent documentation on records, events not immediately connected with his own activities would have meant little to him; but it is doubtful whether we would have approved of the flowering of New Orleans music that followed his brief new lease of life and that might not have taken place without his magnetism to give it its initial momentum.

It is ironic that Bunk should now be so closely associated with

116

the so-called New Orleans Revival. Had he lived longer he would probably have wanted little part in it, but would have continued to look for work in the North, where the attitude was more sophisticated and the musicianship less instinctive. Those of us who have found so much to enjoy in the playing of the latter-day New Orleans musicians must, however, be profoundly grateful to Bunk, as well as to those who supported him during his comeback, for making it all possible. We must also remember and be grateful for his much earlier influence on some of the great men of the classic period of jazz, and wonder just how the music would have developed without his guiding hand during its evolutionary phase.

Whether Bunk was a sincere, straightforward man who was unfortunate in his dealings with some of his associates, or whether he was a con-man, a ruthless opportunist and even a downright liar, we must accept that all his efforts were directed towards an ultimate musical result. Coming from a background where hustling was necessary for survival, let alone for success in music, he may well have felt that any means justified his ends. It is certainly safe to say that, without his strongly egotistical character, he would not have been the musician he was, and would probably not have achieved as much as he did without an inherent aggressive single-mindedness. This did not make him easy to live with, and it may have been his tragedy that ultimately he pushed too hard in company that, up to a point, was only too happy to accommodate him. If he was misunderstood it was at least partly his own fault; but there were those who were only too willing to misunderstand him, and to characterize him with interests and motives more appropriate to a middle-class white man. With hindsight, we can hear a good deal more than they were able to hear and place it in its proper context. Whatever else he may have been, Bunk Johnson was a musician, and an accomplished and influential one. We must be everlastingly glad that he was.

BIBLIOGRAPHY

Allen, Walter C. and Brian A. L. Rust	*King Joe Oliver* (Belleville, N.J., 1955) (also Jazz Book Club)
Armstrong, Louis	*Satchmo: My Life in New Orleans* (New York, 1954; London, 1955) (also Jazz Book Club)
Asbury, Herbert	*The French Quarter: An Informal History of the New Orleans Underworld* (New York, 1936; London, 1937)
Barker, Danny	*A Life in Jazz* edited by Alyn Shipton) (London and New York, 1986)
Bechet, Sidney	*Treat it Gentle: An Autobiography* (edited by D. Flower) (New York and London, 1960)
Bethell, Tom	*George Lewis: A Jazzman from New Orleans* (Berkeley, Calif. and London 1977)
Blesh, Rudi	*Shining Trumpets: A History of Jazz* (New York, 1946, rev. and enlarged 2/1958)
Charters, Samuel B.	*Jazz, New Orleans, 1885-1963: An Index to the Negro Musicians of New Orleans* (New York, 2/1963)
Chilton, John	*Who's Who of Jazz: Storyville to Swing Street* (London, rev. and enlarged 4/1985)
Chilton, John	*Sidney Bechet, The Wizard of Jazz* (London, 1987)
Dodds, W. and Larry Gara	*The Baby Dodds Story* (Los Angeles, 1959)
Gillis, Frank J. and John W. Miner, eds.	*Oh, Didn't He Ramble: The Life Story of Lee Collins* (Urbana, Ill., Chicago and London, 1974)

Gammond, Peter — *Scott Joplin and the Ragtime Era* (London, 1975)

Hentoff, Nat and Albert J. McCarthy, eds. — *Jazz: New Perspectives on the History of Jazz by Twelve of the World's Foremost Jazz Critics and Scholars* (New York and Toronto, 1959) (also Jazz Book Club)

Hodes, Art and C. Hansen, eds. — *Selections from the Gutter: Jazz Portraits from "The Jazz Record"* (Berkeley, Calif., and London, 1977)

Jones, Max and John Chilton — *Louis: The Louis Armstrong Story, 1900-1971* (Boston and London, 1971)

Jones, Max — *Talking Jazz* (London, 1987)

Koenig, Karl — *Jazz Map of New Orleans* (New Orleans, 1975)

Lomax, Alan — *Mister Jelly Roll: The Fortunes of Jelly Roll Morton, New Orleans Creole and "Inventor of Jazz"* (New York, 1950, 2/1973) (also Jazz Book Club)

Maestri, Robert (Sponsor) — *New Orleans City Guide* (Boston, 1938)

Marquis, Donald M. — *In Search of Buddy Bolden, First Man of Jazz* (Baton Rouge, La. and London, 1978)

Miller, Henry — *The Air-conditioned Nightmare* (Norfolk, Conn., 1945)

Miller, Paul Edward and Ralph Venables — *Esquire's Jazz Book* (London, 1947)

Miller, William — *A Short History of the United States* (New York, 1969)

Ramsey, Frederic Jr, and Charles Edward Smith — *Jazzmen: The Story of Hot Jazz Told in the Lives of the Men Who Created It* (New York, 1939) (also Jazz Book Club)

Rose, Al and Edmond Souchon — *New Orleans Jazz: A Family Album* (Baton Rouge, La., 1967, rev. and enlarged 3/1984)

Rose, Al — *Storyville, New Orleans: Being an Authentic, Illustrated Account of the Notorious Red-Light District* (University, Ala., 1974)

Rose, Al — *I Remember Jazz* (Baton Rouge, La., and Wellingborough, England, 1987)

Rosenthal, George. S. and Frank Zachary, eds. — *Jazzways* (London, 1946)

Rust, Brian A. L.   *Jazz Records: A-Z* (London, rev. 3/ 1969, rev. and enlarged 4/1978)

Schafer, William J. and Richard B. Allen   *Brass Bands and New Orleans Jazz* (Baton Rouge, La. and London, 1977)

Shapiro, Nat and Nat Hentoff, eds.   *Hear Me Talkin' to Ya: The Story of Jazz by the Men Who Made it* (New York and London, 1955) (also Jazz Book Club)

Smith, Charles Edward, with Frederic Ramsey Jr., Charles Payne Rogers and William Russell   *The Jazz Record Book* (New York, 1942)

Sonnier, Austin M. Jr.   *Willie Geary "Bunk" Johnson: The New Iberia Years* (New York, 1977)

Stagg, Tom and Charlie Crump   *New Orleans, the Revival: a Tape and Discography of Negro Traditional Jazz Recorded in New Orleans or by New Orleans Bands, 1937-1972* ([London], 1973)

Stearns, Marshall W.   *The Story of Jazz* (New York, 1956; London, 1957)

Stoddard, Tom and Ross Russell   *Pops Foster: The Autobiography of a New Orleans Jazzman* (Berkeley, Ca. and London, 1971)

Williams, Martin   *Jazz Masters of New Orleans* (New York and London, 1967)

Wright, Laurie   *'King' Oliver* (London, 1987)

Annual Review of Jazz Studies 3 International Association of Jazz Record Collectors

Ashforth, Alden   The Buddy Bolden Photo – One More Time

Barrell, Alan   'Sidney Bechet', *Footnote*, ii/5

Barrell, Alan   'The Last Testament', *Footnote*, xvi/3

Barrell, Alan   'Fragments of Steele', *Footnote*, xvi/5

Barrell, Alan   'B is for Baquet', *Footnote*, xvii/3

Berger, Morroe   'Early New Orleans Jazz Bands', *Jazz Record* (April 1944); reprinted in *Eureka*, ii/1

Bethel, Tom   'The Revival of Bunk Johnson', *Mississippi Rag* (July 1975)

Bowler, Bill and Sima Ruviditch	'New Orleans Memories', *Record Changer* (October 1948)
Casimir, Mike	'Albert Nicholas Talking', *Footnote* iii/5-6
Donder, Jempi de	'Peter Bocage', *Footnote*, xiii/4
Donder, Jempi de	'My Buddy', *Footnote*, xiv/3-4
Donder, Jempi de and Marcel Joly	'Little Henry', *Footnote* xii/1
Drob, Harold	'Bunk Johnson: An Appreciation', *Record Changer* (1952)
Drob, Harold	'Bunk Johnson: His Last Date', *Record Changer* (1952)
Drob, Harold	'A Pilgrimage', *Mississippi Rag* (September 1979)
Ertegun, Ahmet	'Bunk Back at Casino', *Record Changer* (June 1946)
Ertegun, Nesuhi	'A Style and a Memory', *Record Changer* (July 1947)
Finley, Alice (transcriber)	'Bud Scott', *Record Changer* (September 1947)
Goffin, Robert	'Big Eye Louis Nelson', *Jazz Record* (June 1946) reprinted in *Eureka* ii/1
Greenough, Jane (transcriber)	'What Did Ory Say?', *Record Changer* (November 1947)
Gushee, Lawrence	'Would You Believe Ferman Mouton?' *Storyville*, no. 95
Haby, Peter R.	'Alphonse Picou, New Orleans Creole', *Footnote*, xi/5
Hall, Andrew	'Teddy Johnson', *Footnote*, xi/5
Hazeldine, Mike	'"Dear Wynne"', *Footnote*, xv/5
Heide, Karl Gert zur	'Footnotes: Eddie Cherie', *Footnote* iv/6
Heide, Karl Gert zur	'Footnotes: New Orleans, 1944', *Footnote*, v/1-2
Heide, Karl Gert zur	'Footnotes: the Kimballs and Davis', *Footnote*, vii/4
Heide, Karl Gert zur	'Buddy Burns Recalls New Orleans', *Footnote*, viii/5-6
Holmquist, Mats	'Tony Jackson', *Mississippi Rag* (June 1976)
House, S. and D.	'New Iberia 1981', *Footnote*, xiii/1
Jacobson, Catherine	'More Bunk', *Footnote*, xvii/3
Joly, Marcel	'Lionel Ferbos – John Robichaux', *Footnote*, xi/2
Julian, Jane	'Magnolia's Music', *Mississippi Rag* (July 1974)

Kay, George W.	'Remembering Tony Jackson', *The Second Line*, xv/11-12
Koenig, Karl	'Magnolia Plantation: History and Music', *The Second Line*, xxxiv
Larsen, Paul A.	'Bunk' (letter), *Jazz Journal* (April 1967)
Larsen, Paul A.	'King Oliver–Lizzie Miles Date', *Jazz Report*, vii/2
Larsen, Paul A.	'Bunk is History', *Storyville*, no. 43
Martyn, Barry	'Gus Statiras From Jersey City', *Footnote*, xv/6
Miller, Punch	Interview: Tulane University Jazz Archive (1959)
Miller, Ralph W.	'Carl Davis: Jazz Profile', *Jazz Report*, v/4
Milward, Richard	'Harold "Duke" Dejan', *Footnote* vi/5
Morand, Herb	Interview: Tulane University Jazz Archive (1950)
Napoleon, Art	'The Music Goes Round and Round', *Storyville*, no. 37
Napoleon, Art	'Aw: Get a Piccolo', *Storyville*, no. 39
Norris, John	'Paul Barbarin', *Eureka*, i/1
Paddon, John	'Hypolite Charles', *Footnote*, xii/4
Page, Len	'I Thought I Heard Buddy Bolden Play', *Footnote* xviii/4
Reid, John D.	'Bechet and Bunk in Boston', *The Second Line*, xxiv
Ridley, Andy	'Louis Keppard', *Storyville*, no. 40
Russell, William	'Albert Nicholas Talks about Jelly Roll', *The Second Line*, xxix, xxx
Sancton, Thomas	'Glenny: Stone Age Man of Jazz', *Eureka*, 1/2; reprinted in *The Second Line* (April 1951)
Slingsby, John	'New Orleans Horns', *Eureka*, i/2
Smith, Charles Edward	'Clarence Williams', *Record Changer* (April 1948)
Smith, Charles Edward	'The Buddy Bolden Cylinder', *Eureka*, i/2
Sonnier, Austin	'Lawrence Duhé', *Footnote*, xiii/5
Sonnier, Austin	'Jazz Talk: Harold Potier and Morris Dauphine', *Footnote*, xiv/3
Sonnier, Austin	'The Banner Orchestra', *Footnote*, xviii/3
Souchon, Edmond	'Long-Gone-but-Not-Forgotten', *The Second Line*, xv/5-6
Souchon, Edmond	'Weeks Hall and Bunk Johnson', *The*

	Second Line, xv/9-10
Stagg, Tom	'Eddie Dawson and Sylvester Handy', *Footnote*, iv/2
Stagg, Tom	'Facts and Fancies', *Footnote*, iv/5
Stagg, Tom	'Glimpses into the Past', *Footnote*, vi/3
Standish, Tony	'Joseph Robichaux: those Early Days', *Jazz Journal* (April 1959)
Standish, Tony	'Outlook', *Eureka*, i/3
Tovey, Mike	'Kid Thomas Valentine', *Footnote*, xi/1
Tovey, Mike	'On the Banquette: Joe Johnson', *Footnote*, xi/2-3
Tovey, Mike	'On the Banquette: Bunk and Bechet', *Footnote* xi/4ff
Tovey, Mike	'On the Banquette: Tig Chambers', *Footnote*, xi/5; xii/2
Vorst, Paige Van	'Eight Years in a Barrelhouse', *Misissippi Rag* (September 1974)
Wiatt, Alexander	'An Interview with Earl Humphrey', *Jazz Report*, v/1ff
Walker, Edward S.	'Bunk Johnson in England', *Storyville*, no. 49
Wittrick, Rae	'Lee Collins 1901-1960', *Eureka*, i/4
Wittrick, Rae (transcriber)	'Bunk Johnson Interview', *Eureka*, ii/1

INDEX